Life from Light

Saints Along The Way

Leo Osborn

McKnight & Bishop Ltd
Inspire

ISBN 978-1-905691-31-9

A CIP catalogue record for this book is available from the British Library

First published in 2014 by McKnight & Bishop Inspire, an imprint of:

> McKnight & Bishop Ltd.
> 28 Grifffiths Court, Bowburn, Co. Durham, DH6 5FD
> http://www.mcknightbishop.com
> info@mcknightbishop.com

This books has been typeset in Garamond, Ǒк Northumbria and Celtic MD.

Printed and bound in Great Britain by The Printing House, London.

The paper used in this book has been made from FSC approved wood independently certified as having come from sustainable forests. The inks used are vegetable & soy based, making this book more environmentally friendly, providing more accurate colour reproduction and making this book easier to recycle.

About The Publisher

McKnight & Bishop are always on the lookout for great new authors and ideas for exciting new books. If you write or if you have an idea for a book, email us:

info@mcknighbishop.com

Some things we love are: undiscovered authors, open- source software, crowd-funding, Amazon/Kindle, social networking, faith, laughter and new ideas.

Visit us at: www.mcknightbishop.com

This book is dedicated to all the Saints of God in the
Newcastle upon Tyne Methodist District
whom it has been a privilege to live and serve among.

For Charlotte
who has shared my journey,
enriched my life
and reflected the light of Jesus.

Copies of this book are free but
donations are welcome for the work of

ALL
WE
CAN

Methodist
relief and
development

Introduction

Since I was a child I have loved walking and exploring new places. When I became older I valued "getting away from it all" and getting a little fitter at the same time. In more recent years however my walking has taken a different focus as I have journeyed along pilgrim paths sometimes on my own and sometimes in the company of friends. Often these have been in Northumbria - St. Cuthbert's, St. Oswald's and Bede Way for example or following in the footsteps of the monks from Lindisfarne to Monkwearmouth and John Wesley through The Dales of County Durham and North Yorkshire but sometimes I have journeyed further afield - along the Whitby Way, the Cornish Way and the last part of the Spanish route to Santiago de Compostela. There have also been times when the walk has not been to a place of pilgrimage but in a place of pilgrimage and time spent in Assisi, Avila, Fatima, Medjugorje, Norwich, Prague, Rome, Segovia, Walsingham or in the steps of St Paul in Greece have been rich experiences. And as I've walked I've encountered saints. Sometimes of course the saint is in the name of the walk itself and some of these feature in what follows but there are numerous other saints who have come to mind and who have enriched my spiritual journey thus far and they are here too. Some will be well known - from the Bible or the pages of Church History, others may be quite unfamiliar to you as they were to me and still others may seem surprising choices, but they are saints to me in the widest and I believe Biblical sense of that word. For my working definition of a saint is not simply one who is found in a stained glass window but everyone whom God's light shines through.

So the purpose of this booklet is three fold. First to reflect further on the Saints who have been a part of my journey and not least those whom the church celebrates in the period from Advent to Candlemas; Light as it were from Light. As the years go by their presence within The Communion of Saints has become more and more life-enhancing and faith-enhancing and I thank God for them. Second, to help you reflect not simply on "my" saints but on your saints. I hope this booklet will help you find them and thus encourage you on your journey as you follow their God and yours. Third it is to speak to us all of the paradox that all Christians are saints even whilst still sinners. So I pray these reflections will remind us of what we already are, and enable us to become, by God's grace, what we are called to be.

Prayer

For all the saints who showed your love
in how they lived and where they moved,
for mindful women, caring men,
accept our gratitude again.

For all the saints who loved your name,
whose faith increased the Saviour's fame,
who sang your songs and shared your word,
accept our gratitude, good Lord.

For all the saints who named your will,
and saw your kingdom coming still
through selfless protest, prayer and praise,
accept the gratitude we raise.

Bless all whose will or name or love
reflects the grace of heaven above.
though unacclaimed by earthly powers,
your life through theirs has hallowed ours.

John L. Bell (b. 1949) and Graham Maule (b. 1958)

Leo Osborn
Sabbatical in Norfolk
(Advent 2013 – Candlemas 2014)

December 1st ~ Advent

Therefore, since we are surrounded by such a great cloud of witnesses, let us throw off everything that hinders and the sin that so easily entangles. And let us run with perseverance the race marked out for us, fixing our eyes on Jesus, the pioneer and perfecter of faith. For the joy set before him he endured the cross, scorning its shame, and sat down at the right hand of the throne of God.

Hebrews 12 vv 1-2a

Reflection

So many themes are brought together on the first Sunday in Advent - waiting, watching, hope, readiness and of course light. And because they are all to do with looking forward they usually gel quite well even if it is not always clear whether we are waiting for Christmas, watching for Christ's return or celebrating the hope He brings to the world as He comes to us in others.

The women and men of faith (or the Saints along the Way) mentioned in Hebrews 11 and 12 were certainly looking forward (or looking forward certainly) as well - to the heavenly city, that place where God dwells with His people and to that time when we with them would share its joy. As they look forward still so they look out for us, and to Jesus the Alpha and Omega of faith, to bring us safely home.

So:

What are you looking forward to this Advent?

Who are you looking out for?

Prayer

Almighty God,
Give us grace to cast away the works of darkness
and to put on the armour of light,
now in the time of this mortal life,
in which your Son Jesus Christ
came to us in great humility:
that, on the last day,
when He shall come again in his glorious majesty
to judge the living and the dead,
we may rise to the life immortal;
through Him who is alive and reigns with you,
in the unity of the Holy Spirit,
one God, now and for ever. Amen

Collect for the First Sunday in Advent

Isaiah was an Old Testament prophet of 8th century B.C. It is very likely that he began his career as a priest in the temple of Jerusalem. There he saw a vision and received his prophetic call. (Isaiah 6) His ministry lasted at least forty years and his words were so influential that he inspired others to write in his name. Countless generations continue to be inspired through his words not least as they have been set to music by Handel in Messiah - a way in which for many Advent begins.

Reflection

The call of Isaiah has always been important to me for although my call to ministry came in a quite different way to his - that sense of awe, unworthiness, forgiveness, acceptance, commissioning and response is certainly one I can identify with. More recently to hear these words read at each ordination at which I have presided, preached or assisted, and to reflect on the way in which God's call to Isaiah has been heard afresh by each ordinand, has been profoundly moving.

Yet despite the "comfortable" words of his prophecy about swords being beaten into ploughshares, wolves living with lambs and light shining in darkness (see chapters 2, 9 & 11), his was a message of denunciation as well as annunciation. By trusting in military alliances, bowing down to the idols of security and affluence and oppressing the poor, those to whom he was writing were losing sight of their dependence on God. The result would be disaster and all their fine sacrifices and many prayers would not save them. The promise of a future Messiah and of a peaceable Kingdom remained but it would be many centuries before it was fulfilled in part and still we wait for its final coming.

So:

Who has spoken "comfortable" words to you at a time you needed to hear them?

Who has spoken words to you which you did not wish to hear? Were they justified? If so be thankful for their wisdom and courage.

Prayer

> *Christ our Advent hope,*
> *bare brown trees,*
> *etched dark across a winter sky,*
> *leaves fallen, rustling,*
> *ground hard and cold,*
> *remind us to prepare for your coming,*
> *remind us to prepare for the time*
> *when the soles of your feet will touch the ground,*
> *when you will become one of us*
> *to be at one with us. Amen*

Kate McIlhagga

December 3ʀᴅ ~ Francis Xavier

Francis was born at the castle of Xavier in Spanish Navarre in 1506. He was educated in Paris and with Ignatius of Loyola, became one of the group of seven who took vows as the first members of the Society of Jesus, or Jesuits. Since preaching the gospel overseas was an integral part of the Jesuit vocation, Francis sailed for Goa, on the west coast of India in 1541. He travelled all over the East Indies, evangelising and establishing the Church in Ceylon, Malacca, Malaya and notably in Japan, where he left behind two thousand converts. He had just reached China when he died on board ship in December 1552.

Reflection

Francis Xavier was just a name to me but as I've read a little of his life I've reflected on how the church in China and indeed in South Korea has grown from such inauspicious beginnings. Francis Xavier died on board ship before he ever set foot in China and Methodist missionaries to South Korea were likewise massacred as they disembarked with only a fragment of one gospel floating ashore. In a few months' time however I shall have the privilege of visiting Amity Publishing in Nanking where 3.5 million copies of the Bible are produced each year for the people of China hungry for the word of God and I recall how twenty years ago I spent time in South Korea visiting some of the largest congregations in the world and re-learning some of the principles of mission which we had inherited from John Wesley two centuries before! So the verse that the Newcastle upon Tyne District is focusing on this year reminds us not to despise the day of small things (Zechariah 4 v10) for as the saying goes: "mighty oaks from tiny acorns grow".

So:

What are the seemingly small things that you do today which in God's good time may become great things? Offer them to God.

What random acts of kindness shown to you by Saints along the Way cause you to give thanks to God?

Prayer

> *My God I love you not because I hope for heaven thereby or of gaining a reward but because you have first loved me and embraced me upon the cross in Jesus Christ.*
> *Amen*

> *Francis Xavier (Adapted)*

December 4th ~ Saint Chad

Chad was born in Northumbria, the youngest of four sons, all of whom became both priests and monks. They entered the monastery on the Isle of Lindisfarne and were taught by St Aidan. Chad's brother Cedd had founded the abbey at Lastingham and on his brother's death, Chad was elected abbot and became Bishop of York for a time, but he graciously stepped back with the arrival in Britain of Theodore, who doubted the validity of indigenous consecrations. This was eventually rectified and Chad became Bishop of Mercia, a huge diocese the centre of which he moved to Lichfield. Chad travelled extensively and became much loved for his wisdom and gentleness in otherwise difficult situations. The plague was prevalent at this time and Chad died on this day in the year 672.

Reflection

Choral Evensong on Radio 3 today came from Lichfield, a Cathedral I know well not least because as a child I used to be taken to see the altar frontals that my Great Aunt had made! Lichfield Cathedral, like the Roman Catholic Cathedral in my home city of Birmingham, is dedicated to St. Chad but it was only recently when I was walking the Whitby Way at the beginning of my sabbatical that I realised I was following in the footsteps of St. Chad himself. Visiting the crypt and church at Lastingham where Chad was Abbot had a profound effect on me and I was determined to find out more about him. Reading between the lines there seems at best to have been some confusion surrounding the respective claims of Wilfred and Chad to be Bishop of York. At worst skulduggery may not have been far below the surface. But Chad, aware of the disrepute such a potential conflict might bring both to the church and His Lord, simply stepped back and gave way. We can't know what this cost him personally, although I imagine it must have been considerable. What we do know is that he was following in the footsteps of Christ, who as the collect for the First Sunday in Advent proclaims, 'came to us in great humility.'

So:

What are the authentic marks of Christian humility in 21st century?

When did you last step back or give way for the good of others or the sake of Christ?

Prayer

> Almighty God,
> from the first fruits of the English nation
> who turned to Christ,
> you called your servant Chad
> to be an evangelist and bishop of his own people:
> give us grace so to follow his peaceable nature,
> humble spirit and prayerful life,
> that we may truly commend to others
> the faith which we ourselves profess;
> through Jesus Christ your Son our Lord,
> Amen

December 5th ~ Rosalie Periam

Rosalie Periam was born in 1918 in Solihull and died in Cambridge in 2001. Although she only worked at Kew gardens for a short period her interest in horticulture was a lifelong one. In later years she worked in a guest house and cared for her Mother and in retirement enjoyed holidays by the sea, sketching, dress-making, entertaining students away from home for the first time, spending time with family and friends and making gifts for birthdays and Christmas.

Reflection

At one level you couldn't find a more ordinary life than that led by Rosalie Periam. She had no great ambitions, little interest in material things and superficially achieved very little but she was my Aunt who I got to know and love very much and I know how much her life counted in the eyes of others. Her appreciation of and fascination in God's world, her deep interest and concern for people, her daily prayers for each member of her extended family (which was large!) all stemmed from her deep love for God and her simple trust in Jesus Christ. Rosalie never married which I suspect was a deep sadness to her but she channelled her love in a different direction and there are so many who were influenced by her life for good and not a few who trace their coming to faith and to growing in faith to her. Her eccentric ways earned her the nickname of the Mad Aunt, which she played up to for all she was worth and although some thought her foolish rather than mad for living as she did, her life is a reminder that The Gospel to many is foolishness but nevertheless the way that God has chosen to bring salvation to the world. As we gave thanks for her life in December 2001 it was my privilege to preach on the foolishness and wisdom of God shown so wonderfully in His servant Rosalie Periam!

So:

How wise and foolish are you in human eyes and in God's eyes?

What ordinary person who did extraordinary things for God are you thankful for today?

Prayer

From Rosalie Periam's favourite hymn

> *May the mind of Christ my Saviour*
> *live in me from day to day,*
> *by his love and power controlling*
> *all I do or say.*
>
> *May the peace of God my Father*
> *rule my life in everything,*
> *that I may be calm to comfort*
> *sick and sorrowing.*
>
> *May the word of God dwell richly*
> *in my heart from hour to hour,*
> *so that all may see I triumph*
> *only through his power*
>
> *May the love of Jesus fill me,*
> *as the waters fill the sea;*
> *him exalting, self-forgetting —*
> *this is victory.*

Katie Barclay Wilkinson

December 6ᵗʰ ～ Nelson Mandela

Nelson Mandela was born on 18th July 1918 in a village near Untata in the Transkei. He joined the African National Congress in 1943 and in 1952 opened a law practice in Johannesburg with his partner Oliver Tambo. Together they campaigned against apartheid but in 1960 the ANC was outlawed and Nelson Mandela went underground. Until that time the ANC policy had been one of peaceful resistance but after the Sharpeville massacre in which 69 black people were shot dead, the ANC with Nelson Mandela as Vice President and then President, launched a sabotage campaign. Arrested in 1964 on charges of treason and sabotage he was sentenced to life imprisonment serving 27 years, 18 of them on Robben Island.

On 11th February 1990 after growing international pressure Nelson Mandela was released and within days the ANC and the National Party began talks about forming a new multi-racial democracy for South Africa. In December 1993, with Mr de Klerk, he was awarded the Nobel Peace Prize and five months later was elected South Africa's first black President. He died on 5th December 2013 aged 95.

Reflection

Last night the news came through that Nelson Mandela had died. Was he a saint? Well certainly not in the conventional sense of that word. He was it seems a nominal Christian (and an even more nominal Methodist!) albeit with a strong faith in the ultimate triumph of good over evil. Yet his definition of sainthood was spot on. In speaking of himself he said:- "I'm not a saint unless you think of a saint as a sinner who keeps on trying".

At the end of the World Methodist Council in South Africa in 2011,

I visited Robben Island. It was a cold and misty day which accentuated the distance between the island and the mainland. We were shown round by one of those who had been a prisoner under the apartheid system. Nelson Mandela's tiny and bare cell where he spent much of those 18 years in solitary confinement, the tattered rug of a blanket on which he slept, the quarry in which he smashed rocks when not incarcerated, were each pointed out. This bleak and barren landscape seemed "hopeless" yet from it hope did come through one man who refused to give up believing that one day apartheid would end and a just and fairer society be born but that it would only come about through forgiveness and reconciliation. On his release and subsequently as President, he put those beliefs into practice and inspired others to do the same. In so doing he will always be a mirror in which we see the face of Christ who on the cross prayed "Father, forgive".

So:

Through many years of waiting do I still believe the world can be different and if so how am I demonstrating that?

Who do I need to forgive and be forgiven by?

Prayer

> *Bless our beautiful land O Lord,*
> *with its wonderful variety of people*
> *of races, cultures and languages.*
> *May we be a nation*
> *of laughter and joy,*
> *of justice and reconciliation,*
> *of peace and unity,*
> *of compassion, caring and sharing.*
> *We pray this prayer for a true patriotism,*
> *in the powerful name of Jesus our Lord.*
> *Amen*

> *Archbishop Desmond Tutu*

December 7ᵗʰ ~ St Nicholas

Nicholas was a fourth-century bishop of Myra in Asia Minor (southern Turkey). His reputation as a worker of wonders was enhanced by a ninth-century author of his hagiography and he is now best known through these stories. Many of them concern his love and care for children and so developed the tradition of bearing gifts to children on his feast day, a practice appropriated by the Christmas celebrations. Nicholas is also one of the patron saints of Russia.

Reflection

Officially I'm a day late with Saint Nicholas as he is usually celebrated on 6th December especially in the Netherlands where gifts are given to children in his honour. But the death of Nelson Mandela took precedence and anyway saints are used to having their feast day "transferred"! Around Saint Nicholas there are many stories of generosity some of which may actually be true! In one he rescued three young girls whose father, for want of a dowry, was about to sell them into prostitution. By tossing three bags of gold through an open window it was discovered there was just enough to pay for the dowry of each. In another he wanted to help a poor family but did not want them to know it was him. So he climbed up to their roof on Christmas Eve and dropped some coins down the chimney. The next morning the coins, to the great surprise of the family, were found in the stockings which had been hanging there to dry by the fire the night before! And from such stories the giving of presents and the hanging of stockings has become a part of a "traditional" Christmas the world over. However Saint Nicholas might best be remembered not only as the 4th century equivalent of Father Christmas but also as the protector of those whose lives and innocence remain threatened today as they were in his own time by violence, poverty and exploitation.

St Paul writes: "You know the generous act of our Lord Jesus Christ that though he was rich yet for your sakes He became poor so that by His poverty you might become rich" (2 Corinthians 8 v 9). St. Nicholas was one who took such words to heart as he sought to follow in Christ's footsteps.

So:

How have you experienced the generous act of the Lord Jesus Christ in your life?

To whom will you be generous this Christmas?

Prayer

> *Almighty Father, lover of souls,*
> *who chose your servant Nicholas*
> *to be a bishop in the Church,*
> *that he might give freely out of the treasures of your grace:*
> *make us mindful of the needs of others*
> *and, as we have received, so teach us also to give;*
> *through Jesus Christ your Son our Lord,*
> *who is alive and reigns with you,*
> *in the unity of the Holy Spirit,*
> *one God, now and for ever.*
> *Amen*

December 8th ~ hilda of Whitby

Hilda was born in the year 614 of the royal house of Northumbria and was baptised in York at the age of twelve by Paulinus. Encouraged by Aidan of Lindisfarne, she became a Religious at the age of thirty-three. She established monasteries first at Hartlepool and two years later at Whitby. This house became a great centre of learning and was the meeting place for the important Synod of Whitby in the year 664 at which it was decided to adopt the Roman tradition in preference to Celtic customs. Although herself a Celt in religious formation, Hilda played a crucial role in reconciling others of that tradition to the decision of the Synod. She is also remembered as a great educator, exemplified in her nurturing of Caedmon's gift of vernacular song. She died in the year 680.

Reflection

I completed my 66 mile walk from York to Whitby today and as I arrived at the abbey built by Hilda, thought of all those who had made the same pilgrimage and arrived at the same destination on their way to the Synod in 664. It was an overwhelming feeling of continuity with the Saints of God from centuries past.

Hilda was a remarkable woman. To have presided over the Synod of Whitby attended by Kings and Bishops have led some to believe that Hilda must have been a Bishop herself - an attractive though unlikely thought! Despite her considerable gifts and no doubt forceful character as abbess and educator it was Hilda who graciously and patiently worked with those who found the decision to follow Roman rather than Celtic practice difficult, encouraging them to "come on board" even though she herself might well have preferred the Celtic way of doing things. But in laying aside her personal preferences Hilda played a crucial role in holding the church together when it was in acute danger of schism. It is for this as well as for all her many other gifts that she should best be remembered.

So:

What does it mean for you to prefer others' needs?

What is it worth compromising over for the sake of unity?

Prayer

> Grant me, O Lord, to know what is worth knowing, to love what is worth loving, to praise what delights you most, to value what is precious to you, and to reject whatever is evil in your eyes. Give me true discernment, so that I may judge rightly between things that differ. Above all, may I search out and do what is pleasing to you, through Jesus Christ our Lord.
> Amen

Thomas à Kempis

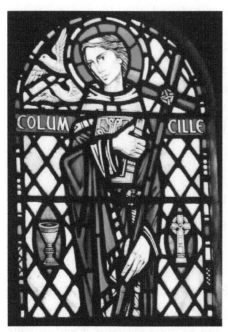

Born in Ireland in about the year 521, Columba was trained as a monk by St Finnian and then founded several monasteries himself, including probably that of Kells, before leaving Ireland to settle on Iona off the coast of Scotland. He was accompanied by twelve companions and the number grew as the monastic life became more established and well-known. Columba seems to have been an austere and at times harsh man who reputedly mellowed with age. He was concerned with building up both the monastery and its life and of enabling them to be instruments of mission in a heathen land. He converted kings and built churches, Iona becoming a starting point for the expansion of Christianity throughout Scotland. In the last four years of his life, when his health had failed, he spent the time transcribing books of the gospels for them to be taken out and used. He died in the year 597.

Reflection

I had always wanted to visit Iona, partly because everyone who had been said what a "thin place" it was in terms of spanning earth and heaven and partly because of its significance as a place of pilgrimage for many centuries. I was also aware of its role is sending out missionaries like Aidan and Cuthbert to evangelize much of Northern England and of its on-going missionary work through the Iona Community and its worship resources. In September 2013 I was able to fulfil my ambition and although the journey was arduous and my stay short it was a special time made even more memorable by the breath-taking scenery.

My knowledge of Columba remained sketchy however and it wasn't until my return that I realised he wasn't "whiter than white" as some have sought to portray him. On being discovered secretly copying Jerome's Psalter and refusing to hand it over to its rightful owner despite the ruling of the King, Columba stirred up trouble to such an extent that a war ensued in which three thousand people lost their lives. But from the ruins of deceit, pride, disobedience and bloodshed came a man transformed by the grace and mercy of God who responded to the call of God - and the rest as they say is history. And in learning all this Columba somehow became a more attractive saint and one I could relate to for it is not the falling that is important but whether we are willing to pick ourselves up, dust ourselves down and with Christ start all over again.

So:

In the Gospel readings for the Second Sunday in Advent John the Baptist tells his hearers to "bear fruit worthy of repentance". What does this mean to you?

Do you have a "holy place"?

Prayer

> Be thou a bright flame before me,
> Be thou a guiding star above me,
> Be thou a smooth path below me,
> Be thou a kindly shepherd behind me,
> Today - tonight - and for ever.
> Amen
>
> Columba

Ðecember 10th ~ Thomas Merton

Thomas Merton was born in France in 1915 and after much unhappiness in his life became a Roman Catholic in 1938, joining the Trappist Abbey of Gethsemane in Kentucky three years later. Although best known for his autobiography 'The Seven Storey Mountain,' Merton came to regret his reference to the monastery as a place set apart and his pious scorn towards the world and its citizens. Rather he came to see that by being in prayer in the monastery he was playing his true part in all the struggles and sufferings of the world. Balancing a life of contemplative prayer and openness to others was never easy for him especially when he was much in demand as a speaker and religious guide and he was often misunderstood by those who wished him either to be more "active" or more "passive". In 1968 Merton accepted an invitation to address an international conference of Christian monks in Bangkok. Afterwards he took a shower and was apparently electrocuted as a result of faulty wiring, so fulfilling a "prophecy" recorded in the last words of his autobiography. He died on this day aged 53.

Reflection

Much as I like silence I have never found contemplation at all easy. My mind easily wanders and perhaps I am too much like my Father who in response to Frederick Faber's hymn, 'My God how wonderful Thou art,' and the line 'To gaze and gaze on Thee,' used to say, 'What a waste of time that would be, I want to be busy!' But through the writings of Thomas Merton I have not only come to realise that gazing on God and working for God aren't mutually exclusive but even more important that one feeds off and enriches the other. Furthermore that contemplation takes place best in the midst of life and not apart from it. Which is not to say that I'm any better at it but like countless millions who have been inspired by Thomas Merton's writings, can at least catch a glimpse of its possibilities and a deeper understanding of its value.

So:

What does contemplating on God mean to you?

Is there a balance in your Christian life between activity and stillness?

Prayer

My Lord God, I have no idea where I am going. I do not see the road ahead of me. I cannot know for certain where it will end. Nor do I really know myself, and the fact that I think I am following your will does not mean that I am actually doing so.

But I believe that the desire to please you does in fact please you, and I hope that I have that desire in all that I am doing. I hope that I never do anything apart from that desire. And I know that if I do this you will lead me by the right road though I may know nothing about it.

Therefore I will trust you always. Though I may seem to be lost and in the shadow of death I will not fear, for you are ever with me and you will never leave me to face my peril alone.
Amen

Thomas Merton

December 11th ~ Mary Read

Mary Read was born in Birmingham in 1901 and died there in 1984 aged 83. She worked as an almoner, worshipped at Somerset Road Methodist church Handsworth and lived with her sister for many years. She remained unmarried.

Reflection

Look up Mary Read on Google and you will be disappointed for as far as I am aware not a trace of her life remains, not even a photograph and I would be surprised if more than a couple of folk remember her now. But I do for she is one of my saints!

I only really got to know Mary in her later years when she lived on Soho Road in Handsworth. This was the scene of riots in 1981 and at that time Mary was almost totally deaf and blind and was only able to go out on Sundays when she was transported to church. During the riots her flat was broken into on a number of occasions which must have been frightening in the extreme. To say that Mary never complained would be an exaggeration. She could be awkward at times and what she called bluntness others might have called rudeness. So why a saint? Well perhaps for three reasons. The first was the vibrancy of her faith. She had a personal relationship with Christ and was not afraid to share it in a church where such things were rarely spoken of. As a relatively young Christian it was wonderful to discover someone who I could speak to about my Christian experience and know that we spoke the same language even though we were very different in age. The second was when she knew I had been accepted for training for the Methodist ministry. Mary promised to pray for me each day and whenever I saw her subsequently she would say "I'm still praying!" And I believe she prays still. I cannot calculate the difference those prayers have made to my life and ministry but I know they have and I am deeply grateful. And then indirectly Mary taught me a precious lesson about ministry for I found her one day in tears. When I asked her what the matter was she told me that the minister had called on her. Having ascertained that he hadn't upset her I discovered the reason for her tears was that he had spent the visit putting her coal in the coal house after it had been dumped (without sacks) in her back yard. This minister was not altogether liked in the church and lacked the charisma of his predecessor and successor but I learnt that day that practical care and servanthood is at the heart of ministry.

So I thank God for Mary, perhaps the most unsung and certainly the most unknown of the saints in this book but one who has arguably had the greatest influence upon me.

So:

Which unlikely person has had a major influence on your Christian life?

Who are you praying for each day?

Prayer

> Trust in God. Let nothing disturb you,
> Let nothing frighten you.
> All things pass; God never changes.
> Patience achieves all it strives for.
> He who has God finds he lacks nothing,
> God alone suffices.
> Amen
>
> > Teresa of Avila

December 12ᵗʰ ~ John Wesley

Born at Epworth Rectory in Lincolnshire, John Wesley was the son of an Anglican clergyman and a Puritan mother. He entered Holy Orders and following a "heart-warming" experience in 1738 began an itinerant ministry which recognised no parish boundaries. This resulted after his death, in the development of a world-wide Methodist Church. His spirituality involved an Arminian affirmation of grace, frequent communion and a disciplined corporate search for holiness. His open-air preaching, concern for education and for the poor, liturgical revision, organisation of local societies and training of preachers provided a firm basis for Christian growth and mission in England. John died in 1791.

Reflection

In his journal for this day in 1742 John Wesley wrote concerning his time in Newcastle:- "I never felt so intense cold before. In a room where a constant fire was kept, though my desk was fixed within a yard of the chimney, I could not write for a quarter of an hour together without my hands being quite benumbed!" Well having spent the last three days travelling between London, Cologne, Norwich and Newcastle itself I'm profoundly grateful that my experience was not the same as Wesley's - although last year it might well have been and perhaps will be again next year! But I've been aware as I have travelled how increasing numbers of people are bitter cold through sleeping rough on our streets, of how food banks and other agencies are running out of supplies in providing hot meals for those in need and that there are others who have a chill in their hearts through bereavement, loneliness or other tragedies that have befallen them. For many at this time of year there is winter but no Christmas.

So despite the coldness he may have felt in his body (especially in Newcastle!) John Wesley - who is the nearest Methodism gets to having an "official" Saint - not only spoke of a warmed heart experience but practised warm-heartedness towards others. On the occasion mentioned above he was in Newcastle to build an orphan house and later he founded a school, campaigned against slavery, wrote on medicine, visited in prison and gave much of his possessions away to those in need - including his wig, which so impressed a young Christian who I met in Cuba that he candidated for the Methodist ministry as a direct result!

So:

How warm is your heart towards others and towards God?

Pray for all who are cold in body mind or spirit this Advent.

Prayer

> Lord, let me not live to be useless.
> Amen
>
> John Wesley

December 13th ~ Samuel Johnson

Samuel Johnson was born in 1709 and is best known as a writer of dictionaries and as a literary editor. Yet in his lifetime he was renowned for his religious beliefs and as a firm supporter of the practice and order of the Church of England. He had been converted to Christianity as a young man after reading William Law's, 'A Serious Call to a Devout and Holy Life,' and his support of the High Church party was unstinting. He died on this day in 1784.

Reflection

Another reason for visiting Lichfield on regular occasions (see 4th December) was to explore the numerous second-hand book shops established there no doubt in honour of Samuel Johnson who was born in that city.

I love books (hard copy rather than electronic!) and only regret that despite numerous attempts to improve I remain a slow reader, but that is partly because like Johnson I love words and enjoy chewing them over and exploring their origins. Words are precious and "a word in season" or a word out of place can be life-changing to its hearers. But words are powerful as well and can sway minds and affect actions. Johnson knew this and although best remembered now for his 'one liners' was referred to in his day as 'The Great Moralist,' a term of affection and honour, for he sought to use words to turn people to the good and to turn them to God. So another great man

of words William Temple used to pray before he got up to speak:-
"Through the spoken word and in the written word may we see Jesus
the living Word". For all who seek to communicate the Christian
Gospel it's not a bad prayer to pray!

So:

What do your spoken and unspoken words convey of the faith you
proclaim?

Pray for all who speak where many listen – writers, broadcasters,
politicians and preachers.

Prayer

*Almighty God, the giver of wisdom, without whose help
resolutions are vain, without whose blessing study is ineffectual;
enable me, if it be thy will, to attain such knowledge as may
qualify me to direct the doubtful, and instruct the ignorant; to
prevent wrongs and terminate contentions; and grant that I may
use that knowledge which I shall attain, to thy glory and my
own salvation, for Jesus Christ's sake.*
Amen

Samuel Johnson

December 14ᵗʰ — John of the Cross and Teresa of Avila

Born to an impoverished noble family near Avila in Spain in 1542, Juan de Yepes worked as a nurse and received further education from the Jesuits before entering the Carmelite order when he was twenty-one. He was ordained in 1567 and met Teresa of Avila soon afterwards. He made a great impression on her and she persuaded him to help with her reform of the Carmelite order. His labours brought him into conflict with the religious authorities and he was even imprisoned for a period, yet these experiences prompted some of his finest poetry and mystical writing. In particular he described the 'dark night' of the soul as it is purified in its approach towards God. After a severe illness he died on this day in 1591.

Teresa was born into an aristocratic Spanish family in 1515. Following her mother's death she ran away from home to enter a Carmelite convent when she was twenty. After initial difficulties in prayer, her intense mystical experiences attracted many disciples. She was inspired to reform the Carmelite rule and assisted by John of the Cross she travelled throughout Spain founding many new religious houses for men as well as women. She knew great physical suffering and died of exhaustion in 1582.

Reflection

In October this year I was privileged to visit Northern Spain with other North East Church Leaders. We stayed at the English College in Valladolid and were overwhelmed by their welcome and generosity and enjoyed immensely our prayer times together and the time to get to know each other better. We visited Avila on Teresa's feast day (an experience in itself!) and also Segovia where John spent much of his time, and had the opportunity to learn more of their life and teaching - in my case learning more wasn't difficult! So amongst other things I came to appreciate Teresa's boldness and sense of humour. On one occasion she couldn't avoid complaining to Jesus about the hostility and gossip that surrounded her. When He told her:- "Teresa that's how I treat my friends" she responded "No wonder you have so few of them then!" and on another occasion thanked John for answering a question she hadn't asked "like all religious teachers especially men!" I also learnt that "the dark night of the soul" that John experienced was not so much to do with a sense of separation from God or of doubt, depression etc. as is often thought but a means whereby the spiritual life is deepened, our need of God magnified and our preciousness to Him made clearer than ever before.

And it is this sense of our preciousness to God who is the lover always looking out for us, delighting in us and overjoyed when we come into His presence that seems to me to be John and Teresa's greatest insight and is such a powerful antidote to the understanding of prayer as duty, demand or drudgery. For if God is really like this who would not want to come in him in love, and to be loved?

So:

Do you find prayer a duty or a delight? Why? What does this say about how you view God?

Give thanks for a sense of humour and those who puncture your pomposity!

Prayer

> Dear Lord, give me the truths which are veiled by the doctrines and articles of faith, which are masked by the pious words of sermons and books. Let my eyes penetrate the veil, and tear off the mask, that I can see your truth face to face. Amen
>
> John of the Cross

December 15th —
Geoffrey Studdert-Kennedy

Born in 1883, Studdert-Kennedy was a young vicar in Worcester who became an army chaplain during the First World War. His warm personality soon earned the respect of soldiers who nicknamed him 'Woodbine Willie' after the brand of cigarettes he shared with them. After the first World War he became a writer and preacher, drawing large crowds who were attracted by his combination of traditional sacramental theology with more unconventional theological views. He worked tirelessly for the Christian Industrial Fellowship but his frail health gave way and he died (still a young man) in 1929.

Reflection

I first came across Geoffrey Studdert-Kennedy as a teenager through the poem "Indifference" in which he contrasted the coming of Jesus to Golgotha with the coming of Jesus to Birmingham and have rediscovered him through reading the latest biography of this remarkable man. For him God was best - perhaps only - encountered in the humanity of Jesus and the humanity of others and it was his own down-to-earthness that so endeared him to many whether in the trenches distributing Woodbines (hence Woodbine Willie) to the troops or in the pulpit or on a platform using earthy language to say profound things.

Studdert-Kennedy had been a strong advocate for the War in 1914 but by its end had come to see its waste and futility. In later years he spoke out increasingly of the need to find a better way to end conflict and heal divisions. As brave in this as he was on the front line, he epitomised the words of one of his few hymns:- "To give and give and give again what God has given thee, to spend thyself nor count the cost, to serve right gloriously the God who gave all worlds that are and all that are to be".

So:

When did you last change your mind on an important matter? Was it a sign of strength or weakness?

In this season of Advent when we prepare for the coming of the King what does the humility of Jesus means to you?

Prayer

> *God who became as we are, may we become as you are.*
> *Amen*
>
> *after William Blake*

December 16th ~ Doris Smith

Doris Smith was born in London on 16th December 1909. She became an officer in the Salvation Army but after marrying her husband who was a Methodist Minister became a Methodist herself and spent much of her life travelling with him to different part of the Connexion whilst exercising her own ministry of preaching and practical care. After his death Doris moved to Lanchester in County Durham and now lives in a residential home in Leadgate a few miles away. On this day she celebrated her 104th birthday.

Reflection

I'm inclined to say that Doris is one of my "own Saints" but that would be too possessive for in reality Doris - or Grannie as she is affectionately known for obvious reasons - is a person who many would say draws you closer to God simply by being in her presence, another good definition of a Saint. She is unceasingly thankful for all the joys of life and unfailing in her appreciation of those who care for her or visit her. Always more ready to listen to others than to talk of herself, she has become a confidante to many and a dispenser of Godly wisdom and sound advice and never will a conversation end without her offering prayer. She will speak often of the joy of knowing Jesus but in the most natural of ways so that you are encouraged to think afresh about what Jesus means to you, but it is all done with a smile and laughter is never far below the surface. Is she perfect? No, not by a long way, as she would readily admit. She can be stubborn and fiercely independent and in the church might I imagine have been both dominant and domineering. But these are not the things you remember, for God's refining grace has been at work in her over many long years. Changing her from glory into glory it has made an indelible mark upon her life and she in turn has left an indelible mark upon the lives of many. As she herself would say "Thanks be to God".

So:

Who are the Doris Smiths in your life?

Do others see you becoming more like Jesus as the years go by?

Prayer

> *Dear Jesus, help us to spread your fragrance everywhere we go. Flood our souls with your spirit and life. Penetrate and possess our whole being so utterly that our lives may only be a radiance of yours. Shine through us, and be so in us, that every soul we come in contact with may feel your presence in our soul. Let them look up and see no longer us but only Jesus! Stay with us, and then we shall begin to shine as you shine; so to share as to be a light to others; the light, O Jesus, will be all from you, none of it will be ours; it will be you, shining on others through us. Let us preach you without preaching, not by words but by our example, by the catching force, the sympathetic influence of what we do, the evident fullness of the love our hearts bear to you.*
> *Amen*
>
> *Cardinal Newman*

December 17th ~ Eglantyne Jebb

Eglantyne Jebb was born in 1876. After studying at Oxford she became a teacher for a few years until ill-health led to her resignation. She then devoted her energies to charitable works and in 1913 went to Macedonia to help refugees in the Balkan wars. After the First World War she and her sister Dorothy Buxton founded the Save the Children Fund, which aimed to help children who were suffering in the post-war famine in Europe, a charity which is now global in its scope. Eglantyne fought for the rights of children to be recognised, the League of Nations passing her 'Children's Charter' in 1924. She inspired many by her personal spirituality and was greatly mourned on her death in Geneva on this day in 1928.

Reflection

My own connection with Eglantyne Jebb is simply that the many hundreds of used stamps I accumulate in any given year – not least at Christmas time – go to Save the Children Fund. But what impressed me particularly in reading about her was her persistence and single-mindedness. Apparently after getting no joy for help from the Archbishop of Canterbury she travelled to Rome and managed to obtain an audience with Pope Benedict XV which lasted for two hours! It's not clear who wore who down but afterwards he issued an encyclical which mentioned Save the Children Fund by name and arranged for collections to be taken in Roman Catholic churches throughout the world on Holy Innocents Day 1919. Shamefacedly the Church of England followed suit and later the Orthodox and

Free Churches. It was such doggedness that eventually led to the Declaration of Geneva covering the rights of children. Sometimes "single issue Christians" can be a blessed nuisance but they get things done and their persistence can help to change the world. Eglantyne Jebb's did.

So:

What are you passionate about?

Pray for children who have no Christmas to look forward to.

Prayer

Written by Save the Children

> Ever-watching Father: we pray for the suffering children whom we do not see. We know that your eyes see their tears, that your heart knows their sorrow, that your hands can reach them now.
> We remember that Jesus was once a child, that poverty stole his bread, that tyrants sought his life, that his mother tasted tears.
> We ask you to send friends for the lonely, food for the hungry, medicine for the sick, saviours for the enslaved, rescue for the perishing.
> Give us the wisdom to do our part, share our possessions, leave our comforts, lend them our voice, send them our food and love them with more than prayers.
> We call on you in the name of Your Child Jesus.
> Amen

December 18th ~ Charles Wesley

Charles Wesley was born on this day in 1707. He shared with his brother John the building up of early Methodist societies, as they travelled the country. His special concern was that early Methodists should remain loyal to Anglicanism. He married and settled in Bristol and later in London, concentrating his work on the local Christian communities. His thousands of hymns established a resource of lyrical piety which has enabled generations of Christians to re-discover the refining power of God's love. They celebrate God's work of grace from birth to death, the great events of God's work of salvation and the rich themes of Eucharistic worship, anticipating the taking up of humanity into the divine life. Charles died in 1788.

Reflection

When I preached at Newcastle Cathedral on 18th December 2007 at the 300th anniversary of Charles Wesley's birth I spoke of my amazement in discovering how many of Wesley's hymns used the word "all" (in our present hymn book Singing The Faith nearly 84%). And in almost every case the "all" refers to the universality of God's salvation - "all can be saved". This optimism of grace was for both Wesleys pivotal to their understanding of the gospel and central to their preaching. It wasn't welcomed of course by those who believed that God had predestined some to be saved and others by implication to be damned and nor by those who didn't believe it but acted as though they did. If the first of these is not so prevalent today the second is never far away from any of us.

So:

As Christmas approaches what is your attitude to those who only come to church once a year?

Are there any that, consciously or otherwise, you have excluded from your "all"?

Prayer

Answer your mercy's whole design,
my God incarnated for me;
my spirit make your radiant shrine,
my light and full salvation be;
and through the darkened vale unknown
conduct me to your dazzling throne.
Amen

Charles Wesley

December 19th ~ Micah

Micah was a younger contemporary of Isaiah who lived in the Southern Kingdom of Judah in the late 8th century B.C. Little is known about him but his prophecy speaks of God's deep distress at the social ills of the day culminating in one of the purple passages of the Old Testament:- "He has showed you, O people, what is good and what does the Lord require of you? To act justly and to love mercy and to walk humbly with your God" (6 v 8).

Reflection

I have now attended my first carol service and feel pleased with myself that I have been able to delay it for so long! One of the passages traditionally read on these occasions is from Micah and speaks of Bethlehem as the place from which one is to come who is to rule in Israel "whose origin is from of old", which of course Christians have seen as prophesying the coming of Christ.

I have only visited Bethlehem once and my most striking memory is of how I had to bend almost double and bow my head before I could pass through the door into the Church of The Nativity and the supposed birthplace of Christ. As I hear again this Christmas these words of promise for Bethlehem I bow my head in shame at the way Palestinians are being treated there, and in prayer for the diminishing number of Palestinian Christians for whom persecution as well as aggravation is a daily occurrence. May the first words of Micah's prophecy concerning Bethlehem soon be fulfilled:- "They will live securely and He will be their peace".

So:

Which Bible promises are you praying this Advent and for whom?

Is your faith lived on a large map?

Prayer

> *Come, thou long-expected Jesus,*
> *born to set thy people free,*
> *from our fears and sins release us,*
> *let us find our rest in thee.*
>
> *Israel's strength and consolation,*
> *hope of all the earth thou art,*
> *dear desire of every nation,*
> *joy of every longing heart.*
>
> *Born thy people to deliver,*
> *born a child and yet a king,*
> *born to reign in us for ever,*
> *now thy gracious kingdom bring.*
>
> *By thine own eternal Spirit*
> *rule in all our hearts alone;*
> *by thine all-sufficient merit*
> *raise us to thy glorious throne.*
>
> *Charles Wesley*

December 20th ~
George Frederic Handel

George Frederic Handel was born in Halle, Saxony in 1685. He served in the court of the Elector of Hanover before moving to England when the elector was crowned as George 1. His output included 46 operas, 32 oratorios, a large number of cantatas, concerti grossi and other orchestral, instrumental and vocal music. Whilst celebrated for the Water Music and his Music for the Royal Fireworks, it is for Messiah that he has gained most recognition. It was completed in 24 days in 1741 and received its première in Dublin in 1742. A devout Christian, he wrote of his composition "I did think I did see all heaven before me and the Great God Himself" and at the end of his manuscript wrote the letters SDG - Soli Deo Gloria - "To God alone the glory". He died in London in 1759 and is buried in Westminster Abbey.

Reflection

Tomorrow evening I hope to listen to Handel's Messiah in Norwich Cathedral. If Bach is the music of heaven then Handel (with one or two others thrown in) is certainly a good preparation! Music is hugely important to me and enriches my life immeasurably, whether it be through a live concert or CDs at home or in the car. Sacred music particularly speaks to my soul and it would be a poor year if I didn't listen to Messiah and Mendelsohn's Elijah at some point during it. At its best such music becomes for me not simply a case of listening but of worshipping. I trust it will be so again this Christmas.

So:

Which music speaks to your soul? Give thanks to God for it.

"To God alone the glory". How is that worked out in your life?

Prayer

Almighty God whose Son's birth was heralded by angels' song, and whose death for sinners is celebrated in the music of heaven: may we who use our voices to sing your glory also display in our lives the harmony which echoes your praise; through Jesus Christ our Lord.
Amen

Christopher Idle

Original manuscript of Handel's Messiah

December 21ˢᵗ ~ Thomas

Thomas is mentioned among the number of the Apostles in the gospels of Matthew, Mark and Luke but it is in John's gospel that his significance is revealed. Firstly, he is heard encouraging the other disciples to go to Judea with Jesus; then not knowing what Jesus meant when He talked about where He was to go elicited the answer that Jesus was Himself the Way. But probably most famously he was the Apostle notably unconvinced by reports of the Resurrection of Jesus, causing Jesus to show him the marks in His hands and feet and side. Thomas then proclaims the words that have been described as the great climax to John's gospel by saying to Jesus, "My Lord and my God!"

Reflection

It seems strange to celebrate the life of Thomas just four days before Christmas. He is after all more associated with the Resurrection than the Incarnation and historically with doubt rather than faith.

Yet I think the compilers of the lectionary knew what they were doing. For one thing it is important for us to see "The Jesus event" as a whole and not just a show to entertain us at Christmas. Here is not a baby to become soft and sentimental over or imagine stays forever in the manger. This is God made man who in His living, dying and rising again opens the way of salvation to all. So the birth of Jesus is simply the first chapter in the book and is only relevant in the context of the rest of the story. For another thing doubt is an integral part of that first Christmas. It is explicit in Joseph and Mary's response to what is to happen and implicit in the Shepherds and Wise Men. But doubt is not the enemy of faith – what is important is how we deal with it. And despite or because of their doubts each in the story travel on until they see "this thing that has come to pass, and the babe lying in the manger" and kneel and adore. And over thirty years later Thomas makes the same journey of doubt to faith and in an Upper Room rather than a lowly stable makes the same response.

So:

Are doubts and faith in conflict?

Pray for all whose life and faith journey is anything but smooth and straightforward this Christmas.

Prayer

> Christ our light,
> like Thomas we want to see,
> need to touch,
> need to be sure before we believe.
> When we don't know, help us to trust;
> When we can't see, help us to keep on walking.
> Amen
>
> From a New Zealand Prayer Book (adapted)

December 22ᴺᴰ ~ Chico Mendes

Chico Mendes was born in 1944, one of seventeen children. He was the leader of a movement linking the defence of the Amazon region with justice for the poor who lived there. He organised a union of the region's rubber tappers and other poor families who earned their meagre living by extracting the renewable resources of the rain forest. Their future was being threatened by big land owners and ranchers, who preferred to burn and clear the forests to make way for cattle. At first Mendes' aim was simply to protect their rights and livelihood. But his faith led him gradually to expand his concerns to encompass a wider ecological vision. The burning of the forest contributed to "the greenhouse effect". It ruined the land and ultimately threatened the survival of the whole planet. The owners resorted to threats and brutal violence to break the will of the union. But the non-violent tactics of Mendes and his supporters attracted international support. He was called the "Gandhi of the Amazon" and in 1987 the Brazilian government granted reserve status to four areas of the rain forest. A year later on this day Mendes was shot and killed by a rancher and his son.

Reflection

The two major overseas visits I made during my year as President of The Methodist Conference were to Ethiopia and Brazil. In Ethiopia I saw how the Methodist Relief and Development Fund (now All We Can) has enabled nearly two million saplings to be planted to replace the ravages of de-forestation, and in Brazil travelled along the River Amazon on the Methodist Hospital Boat that seeks to provide essential services to the many communities that continue to suffer from the "greenhouse effect." Perhaps Chico Mendes made the connection that the child born in a wooden stable, the man who worked in a carpenter's shop and the Saviour who died on a tree is also the Creator and Carer of all that He has made. So our care and concern for the environment can never be an optional extra but rather is an essential part of our discipleship.

So:

How much do you really care about the world that God has made?

Give thanks for All We Can's work with partners in Ethiopia and for the Methodist Church in Brazil as they seek to right wrongs.

Prayer

> *In a world whose web of life is intricate and beautiful,*
> *save us, Lord, from carelessness and blindness.*
> *In a world whose creatures are so varied and vulnerable,*
> *save us Lord, from plundering and cruelty.*
> *In a world whose waters are fresh and whose oceans should cleanse,*
> *save us, Lord, from wanton polluting.*
> *In a world whose forests protect our air and wild-life,*
> *save us, Lord, from the systems that drive us to destroy them.*
> *In a world whose fruits are rich and plentiful,*
> *save us, Lord, from waste and greed.*
> *Amen*

> *Angela Ashwin*

December 23rd ~ Mary

Nothing for sure is known of the parentage or the place of birth of the Mother of the Lord. Only her name is known for certain - Mary or Miriam (in Hebrew) - and that she had an aged relative called Elizabeth. According to the Gospel of Luke, Mary was a young Jewish girl living in Nazareth, engaged to a man called Joseph, when a messenger from the Lord announced that she was to be the bearer of the Son of God to the world. Her response 'Let it be to me according to your word', and her life of obedience and faithfulness has been upheld ever since as a model for all who hear and obey God's word.

Reflection

I am in danger of becoming schizophrenic about Mary! In my evangelical upbringing she was hardly mentioned or if she was only with warning signs attached! In my pilgrimages to such places as Fatima, Medjugorje or Walsingham she is high and lifted up, requests are made for her special intercession, visions of her are received and revered and theological language like Co-Redemptor, Co-Matrix, Mother of God, Immaculate Conception, Perpetual Virginity and The Assumption are widely used about her. Both of these extremes have their dangers even if ironically each in different ways stress the supremacy of Christ. For myself, although I do not enthrone Mary I honour her deeply as one who despite fear, bewilderment, doubt and perhaps dismay said "Yes" to God both at The Annunciation and over and over again. Her answer was not a foregone conclusion and what God might have done if she had said "No" can only be a matter for conjecture. But her yes helped to fashion our salvation and gave us both an example to follow and also a reminder of what God can still do with our yes today.

So:

What place does Mary have in your thinking and devotions?

What do you need to say "yes" to God about?

Prayer

> *God our Redeemer,*
> *you chose the Virgin Mary,*
> *to be the mother of our Lord and Saviour.*
> *Fill us with your grace*
> *that in all things we may embrace your holy will*
> *and with her rejoice in your salvation;*
> *through Jesus Christ our Lord*
> *who is alive and reigns with you,*
> *in the unity of the Holy Spirit,*
> *one God, now and forever.*
> *Amen*

Francis was born in Assisi in central Italy either in 1181 or the following year. After suffering the ignominy of imprisonment following capture whilst at war with the local city of Perugia, he returned a changed man. He took to caring for disused churches and for the poor, particularly those suffering from leprosy. Whilst praying in the semi-derelict church of St Damian, he distinctly heard the words "Go and repair my church, which you see is falling down and understood this as a call to spiritual as well as material re-building." Others joined him and he prepared a simple, gospel based Rule for them all to live by. As the Order grew, it witnessed to Christ through preaching the gospel of repentance, and emphasising the poverty of Christ as an example for his followers. At his death it had spread throughout western Christendom.

Reflection

St Francis has been back in the news this year with the new Pope naming himself after him but it is probably true that of all the saints Francis has always been most popular not least because of his devotion to animals and simplicity of life-style. But he was also of course the instigator of the Christmas crib - which has blossomed in recent years through numerous crib festivals.

Christmas Eve was always a special day in our home when I was younger, perhaps ever more so than Christmas Day itself. Whilst my

Father would erect the tree and make it ready for the great moment of lighting, my mother would lovingly take the nativity scene figures out of their tissue paper and place them in the stable. It was done quietly, slowly and reverently because for her this was an act of devotion as like Francis she thought of all that the first Christmas meant for each of the characters around the crib. I have so much to thank God for in giving me Christian parents who were in quite different ways both saints of God - but today I thank God especially for the way my Mother taught me not to rush too quickly towards Christmas Day but to pause and wonder and worship on Christmas Eve as I set up my own crib scene.

So:

Do you have a Christmas crib? What does it mean to you?

Jesus was born in a cattle shed and tradition has it that the animals were not removed before Jesus was born. Francis of Assisi reminds us of God's concern for all creatures. What's yours?

Prayer

> *Almighty God,*
> *you make us glad with the yearly remembrance*
> *of the birth of your Son Jesus Christ.*
> *Grant that, as we joyfully receive him as our redeemer,*
> *so we may with sure confidence behold him*
> *when he shall come to be our judge;*
> *who is alive and reigns with you,*
> *in the unity of the Holy Spirit,*
> *one God, now and for ever.*
> *Amen*

Christmas Day

There is only one carol that I am aware of that mentions saints – "Angels from the realms of glory" – and even that reference might be speaking about Christ's first or second coming and is largely based on Old Testament prophecy! But it does highlight the watching that we thought about on Advent Sunday and that we shall return to at Candlemas. Yet both hymn writer and Gospel writers are at one in declaring that it is not so much a day or an event that we are waiting for but the Lord Himself. So although I can understand those who say that the only question worth asking about the Christian faith is "does it work?" it seems to me that you can't avoid John Betjeman's question in his poem Christmas:- "And it is true, and is it true that most tremendous tale of all?"

Indeed it has hit me afresh this Christmas that those who believe it is true and affirmed it at Midnight Mass last night are often the same folk who are today demonstrating that it works through their participation in numerous events for the homeless, lonely or others in need. So it always causes me a wry smile when the largest such event in Norfolk, catering this year for over 500 people, is described as a secular event but is staffed almost entirely by Christians! As I have been doing transport runs back and forth to Open Christmas in Norwich I have been listening to familiar carols on Classic FM but it is the ones that are rarely played yet speak about the meaning of Christmas rather than simply the experience or even the story itself that seem to me to get to the heart of the matter. For the experience fades and the story moves on but the truth remains:- "Our God contracted to a span incomprehensibly made man".

"Love came down at Christmas" I struggle to grasp the wonder of it but I know it's true and because it's true I know it works as well!

So:

Is it true? For you? For all?

How are you living and working out the truth about Christmas?

Prayer

Ever-living God,
whose glory was revealed
in the Word made flesh:
may we, who have seen such splendour
in the coming of your Son,
be true witnesses to your self-giving love in the world;
through Jesus Christ our Lord,
who is alive and reigns with you,
in the unity of the Holy Spirit,
one God, now and for ever.
Amen

December 26th – Stephen

In the book of the Acts of the Apostles, Stephen is described as one of the seven deacons whose job it is to care for the widows in the early Church in Jerusalem. His eloquent speech before the Sanhedrin, in which he shows the great sweep of Jewish history as leading to the birth of Jesus, the long-expected Messiah and his impassioned plea that all might hear the good news of Jesus, leads to his inevitable martyrdom by being stoned to death. He is commemorated on this day.

Reflection

So it's down to earth with a bang! In his Christmas Day sermon Archbishop John Sentamu spoke of Christians being the most persecuted religious group in the world and as though to echo that, news came through later that evening that dozens of church goers in Iraq had been killed when a bomb exploded as they were attending Midnight Mass, and of the increasing privations suffered by Christians in Bethlehem.

But I suppose the martyrdom of Stephen simply asks the question: "Should we be surprised?" for the early church placed his feast day where it did intending surely to imply that the light that shines in the darkness will always be unwelcome to some. So phrases like "comprehended it not, knew Him not, received Him not" in The Gospel Reading for Christmas Day are not only true concerning Jesus the light of the world but to a greater or lesser extent of all who are themselves called to be lights for Him. In truth, down to earth disciples in following a down to earth God!

So:

Stephen saw Jesus standing at the right hand of God (Acts 7 v 56). It's an unusual reference as Jesus is usually described as sitting at God's right hand but presumably Jesus stands up to welcome Stephen into heaven. What does it mean for you to stand up for persecuted Christians in the world today?

Do you face opposition as a Christian? Why? Why not?

Prayer

For the courage of Stephen we thank you,
For the strength to stand up for what we believe we ask you.
For the courage of all who died for you, we thank you,
For the strength to stand firm when the crowd disagrees we ask you.
For the joy of your saints, we thank you,
For delight in the gift of each moment of life we ask you.
Father of mercy, bless our efforts to love you,
and help us, in spite of our uncertainties,
to hear your call, follow your way,
and surrender our lives into your hands.
Amen

Angela Ashwin

December 27th ~ St John

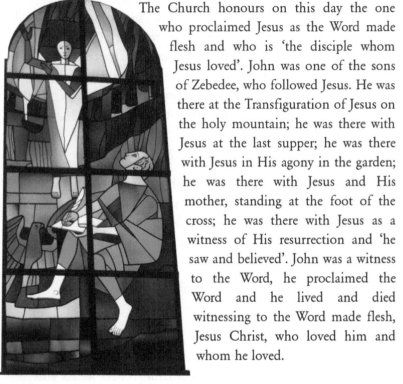

The Church honours on this day the one who proclaimed Jesus as the Word made flesh and who is 'the disciple whom Jesus loved'. John was one of the sons of Zebedee, who followed Jesus. He was there at the Transfiguration of Jesus on the holy mountain; he was there with Jesus at the last supper; he was there with Jesus in His agony in the garden; he was there with Jesus and His mother, standing at the foot of the cross; he was there with Jesus as a witness of His resurrection and 'he saw and believed'. John was a witness to the Word, he proclaimed the Word and he lived and died witnessing to the Word made flesh, Jesus Christ, who loved him and whom he loved.

Reflection

The various portraits that each of the Gospel writers gives us concerning Jesus fascinate me. They are of a piece yet they are subtly different. Matthew highlights His authority, Mark His humility and Luke His suffering but John takes us to a different level – to those parts which the other writers don't reach – to the mystery, meaning, and majesty of God's Son. John's symbol is that of an eagle so he portrays Jesus as the eagle that landed and dwelt among us for a while but has now soared back to heaven where He rules over all things in heaven and earth. All things came into being through Him and all things will find their completion in Him. And the more I read St John's Gospel the more I realise how much there remains for me to understand both of what he writes and the one of whom he is speaking and thus to be stretched and enriched. So if someone wants to know what Jesus did and taught I point them to Matthew. If someone wants to know if Jesus cares and understands about them I point them to Mark. If someone wants to know why Jesus lived and died I point them to Luke. However, if someone wants to know who Jesus was and is, it's in John's direction I invite them to look and find that which is both truth and to be trusted and the One who encapsulates both.

So:

Which Gospel writer "speaks to you" just now?

How is your faith stretched and enriched?

Prayer

Shed upon your church, O Lord, the brightness of your light, that we, being illumined by the teaching of your apostle and evangelist John, may walk in the light of your truth and abide in you for ever;
through Jesus Christ our Lord.
Amen

From The Book of Common Prayer
of the Episcopal Church USA

December 28th – The holy Innocents

Herod 'the Great' was appointed King of the Jews by the Roman authorities in Palestine and he proved to be ruthlessly efficient in his thirty-three years of dealing with his subjects. In Matthew's gospel, he tried to persuade the Magi, to whom he played the host on their journey seeking the one 'who has been born King of the Jews', to bring word of where they had found Him. His desire was to eliminate Jesus and when he realised that the Magi had tricked him and left the country, Herod killed all the children under the age of two in and around Bethlehem.

Reflection

It is an uncomfortable truth that if we take the Gospel accounts as they stand the slaughter of The Innocents would not have happened if Jesus had not been born- and nor indeed would Stephen have been martyred (see December 26th). To say that the end justifies the means or was part of God's plan is at best morally dubious and at worst paints God as the cruellest of puppeteers. Whilst God does undoubtedly bring good out of evil it is hard to justify if God is the catalyst of such evil in the first place!

Yet the mystery of why God allows the innocent to suffer should not blind us to the fact that there is one in this story who is not innocent. Herod was not a puppet who had no say in the matter but faced with light chose darkness. And that is always the choice before us. But it is also our choice when faced with "Holy Innocents" today whether we revert to hand wringing and easy answers or with steadfast faith stand with those who suffer and against those who oppress.

So:

Who are the holy innocents in our world today? Is God found there?

"Christmas is for children." How do you reflect on those words on this day?

Prayer

> Heavenly Father,
> whose children suffered at the hands of Herod,
> though they had done no wrong:
> by the suffering of your Son
> and by the innocence of our lives
> frustrate all evil designs
> and establish your reign of justice and peace;
> through Jesus Christ your Son our Lord,
> who is alive and reigns with you,
> in the unity of the Holy Spirit,
> one God, now and for ever.
> Amen

December 29th ~ Thomas Becket

Thomas Becket was born in London in 1118, of a family of merchants. After a good education he entered the service of Archbishop Theobald of Canterbury. Thomas proved himself an excellent administrator and skilled diplomat. In 1155 he was appointed chancellor by Henry II and they worked harmoniously together in mutual admiration and personal friendship. As a result the king nominated Thomas as Archbishop of Canterbury to succeed Theobald in 1161. From the start there was friction, with Thomas insisting on every privilege of the Church. The conflict worsened until 1164 when Thomas fled to France. Encouraged by the Pope he pursued his arguments from exile, sending letters and pronouncing excommunications. Three efforts at mediation failed before an apparent reconciliation brought him back triumphant to Canterbury in 1170. But the nobility still opposed him and words of anger at court led four knights to journey to Canterbury where they finally chased Thomas into the Cathedral, and murdered him on the steps of the altar on this day in 1170.

Reflection

In the past couple of years the hymn "I vow to Thee my country" has become popular again not least through it being sung at the wedding of William and Kate, the funeral service of Margaret Thatcher, and at various times of remembrance yet it continues to be a cause of controversy not least as a result of the line that reads "The love that asks no questions". Yet Thomas Becket did ask questions about his country and its king and it cost him his life.

Politics is a messy business (and Becket certain wasn't whiter than white in this regard) but the argument that therefore Christians should have no part in it doesn't hold water. Not only is Christianity concerned with the whole of life but more importantly God entered the world in all its messiness at Christmas time (including its political dimension). He came to understand and redeem it and He calls us to share in that work today. Therefore we should give thanks for women and men of courage and commitment like Thomas Becket who in the political sphere and elsewhere are prepared to get their hands dirty. They may not always get it right and we may sometimes profoundly disagree with them but they need our prayers.

So:

What would you say to someone who said "Christianity and politics don't mix?"

How do you engage with the political world?

Prayer

> Lord God,
> who gave grace to your servant Thomas Becket
> to put aside all earthly fear
> and be faithful even to death:
> grant that we, disregarding worldly esteem,
> may fight all wrong, uphold your rule,
> and serve you to our life's end:
> through Jesus Christ your Son our Lord,
> who is alive and reigns with you,
> in the unity of the Holy Spirit,
> one God, now and for ever.
> Amen

December 30th ~ herbert hicks

Herbert Hicks was born in Norfolk in 1913 and lived, worked and worshipped there until his death in 2002. He rarely travelled far from the north of the county living in Knapton for the majority of his life and farming in the locality. He was a Methodist Local Preacher for 68 years, Sunday School Teacher for 40 years, member of the Parish Council for nearly 50 years and of the District Council for 20 years. He also served as Governor of the local school, President of a holiday home for young people and of the Knapton Mens Club, and as Chairman of the Mens Fellowship which he inaugurated. The village sign which he carved is a fitting tribute to him.

Reflection

Herbert is another of "my" saints and not only because he was the "go-between" who enabled Charlotte and me to buy our lovely cottage in Norfolk from where I am writing today! He was a role model to me of consistent Christian living - always the same in church, at home or on the farm. He preached and practised forgiveness, encouraged young people to take on leadership in the life of the church, championed ecumenism and saw the whole of life as both a gift and a trust from God. Towards the end of his life Herbert Hicks said:- "If you feel that I have done something worthwhile or useful in the world I want you to know it was because I loved Jesus Christ". Truly he did and I am so grateful that God gave me the opportunity to know Herbert and to learn afresh that loving Jesus Christ above all else is always the mark of true discipleship.

So:

Who would you like to emulate?

How important do you think consistent Christian living is? Why?

Prayer

Words from Herbert Hicks' favourite hymn

When morning gilds the skies,
my heart awaking cries:
'May Jesus Christ be praised!'
Alike at work and prayer
to Jesus I repair:
'May Jesus Christ be praised!'

Let earth's wide circle round
in joyful notes resound:
'May Jesus Christ be praised!'
Let air, and sea, and sky,
from depth to height, reply:
'May Jesus Christ be praised!'

Does sadness fill my mind?
A solace here I find:
'May Jesus Christ be praised!'
When evil thoughts are near,
these words will calm my fear:
'May Jesus Christ be praised!

Be this while life is mine
my song of love divine:
'May Jesus Christ be praised'
Be this the eternal song,
through all the ages long:
'May Jesus Christ be praised!'

German Hymn – tr. Edward Caswall

December 31ˢᵀ ~ John Wycliffe

John Wycliffe was born in about the year 1330. He was much in favour with members of the royal family and when disputes arose owing to his attacks on the clergy of the day, he was protected by them from the otherwise inevitable consequence of deprivation of his posts. However he went on to deny the Church's teaching of the presence of Christ at the Eucharist, the doctrine known as transubstantiation, and it was this that lost him his royal protection. His opinions were formally condemned in 1381 and he was forced out of office the following year. He had already moved to Lutterworth in 1380 and from there he gave his support to such projects as the translation of the Bible into contemporary English. He died on this day in 1384 whilst at Mass.

Reflection

The name John Wycliffe only consciously came to my notice when one of the members of a previous church I served went to Cameroon with Wycliffe Bible Translators to engage in linguistical work. It was then that I learnt of the painstaking efforts that were being made to translate the Bible not only into languages but dialects, of the many breakthroughs that had already been achieved, of the vast amount of work still to be done and of the extraordinary sacrifices that women and men had made over many years so that "each might hear in their own tongue the wonders of God" (Acts 2). In all this they were following in the footsteps of the one after whom their organisation took its name.

Bible translation through Wycliffe, Bible distribution through The Bible Society, Bible exposition through commentaries, small group material, personal study guides, the preaching of God's Word and of course The Bible itself are precious resources for the church and should never be taken for granted. As with bodily food so with spiritual food – some have so much whilst many still go hungry.

So:

How many Bibles do you have? What are your reflections on that?

Is God's Word still a "lamp to your feet and a light to your path" on the eve of a new year? In what ways?

Prayer

God of revelation,
we thank you that you are not a silent God, isolated from humanity, leaving us to guess and speculate about the things that matter.
We pray for those who serve you by studying manuscripts and clarifying text,
for scholars and preachers who wrestle with the words of life for the building up of your Church,
for linguists, translators and publishers who continue to serve the cause of your Gospel by making the Bible available to more and more people.
Lord create in us a hunger for your Word, a thankfulness for your Gospel, and a faithfulness to your commands, through Jesus Christ our Lord.
Amen

From Patterns and Prayers for Christian Worship

January 1st ~ The Naming and Circumcision of Jesus

The celebration of this festival marks three events: firstly, the naming of the infant; secondly, the sign of the covenant between God and Abraham 'and his children for ever', and thirdly, traditionally the first shedding of Christ's blood. The most significant of these in the gospels is the name itself, which means 'Yahweh saves' and so is linked to the question asked by Moses of God: "What is your name?" "I am who I am," was the reply, thus the significance of Jesus' words: "Before Abraham was, I am." This feast has been observed in the church since at least the sixth century.

Reflection

"At the name of Jesus every knee shall bow" is how the hymn puts it and never more so than in Norwich Cathedral at the Eucharist this morning! It reminded me of an Anglo-Catholic Priest in my first Circuit who would bow deeply whenever he heard the name of Jesus. On one occasion when we sang a modern worship song in which I think the word Jesus occurred eighteen times Albert was more "down" than "up"!

Yet the name Jesus is a special name and one to be honoured and revered which is why I find it hard when it is sometimes used as a swear word not least in the football circles I frequent. But there are other ways in which that name can be dishonoured – through an unwillingness to speak of it for instance or by living in a way that does not do it justice. On this New Year's Day then perhaps the best resolution that any of us might make for our world, our church and our lives is to pray each day "Jesus glorify your name". To live in such a way is the true circumcision of the heart of which the saints spoke and by which they too sought to live.

So:

What does the name of Jesus mean to you?

How do you "name" Him?

Prayer

> In a world of change and hope, of fear and adventure,
> faithful God, glorify your name.
> In human rebellion and obedience, in our seeking
> and our finding,
> faithful God, glorify your name.
> In the common life of our society, in prosperity and need,
> faithful God, glorify your name.
> As your Church proclaims your goodness in words
> and action, faithful God, glorify your name.
> Among our friends and in our homes,
> faithful God, glorify your name.
> In our times of joy, in our days of sorrow,
> faithful God, glorify your name.
> In our strengths and triumphs, in our weakness
> and at our death,
> faithful God, glorify your name.
> In your saints in glory and on the day of Christ's coming,
> faithful God, glorify your name.
> Amen

January 2nd — Basil and Gregory

Basil and Gregory were two friends bound together by their desire to promote and defend the divinity of Christ as proclaimed in the Nicene Creed. This was against the seemingly overwhelming pressure from both Church and State for the establishment of Arianism, which denied Christ's divinity and thus the whole Christian doctrine of the Trinity. Basil was renowned for being headstrong and forceful, in comparison to his friend Gregory, who would rather spend his days in prayer and living the simple ascetic life. Gregory's brilliance in oratory and theological debate meant that a hidden life was virtually impossible and Basil drew him into the forefront of the controversy. Their joint persuasive eloquence convinced the first Council of Constantinople, meeting in 381, that their teaching was the truly orthodox one and the Council ratified the text of the Nicene Creed in the form it is used in the East to this day. Basil died in 379 and Gregory ten years later. They are remembered together on this day.

Reflection

Basil and Gregory (not Pope Gregory of "angels not angles" fame) are saints in the Orthodox tradition which is just as well in the former case for the church opposite my home in Newcastle was only paid for by a rich benefactor on the basis that it could be named after his two sons James and Basil who were killed in the First World War. As a church is traditionally named after saints this caused something of a problem for Basil was not then recognised as a saint in the Western tradition but fortunately the then Bishop of Newcastle remembered that he was in the Eastern tradition and all was well! Basil and Gregory are often spoken of as brothers although in reality they weren't. But such was their affection and regard for each other and their mutual love for the Lord that they came to be spoken of in this way. For the past thirty years or so I have had two brothers like this. We often disagree, we infuriate each other no end, we speak honestly and prick each other's pomposity on regular occasions but I give thanks to God for their unconditional love, continual encouragement, deep wisdom and unending patience and loyalty. Without them my Christian life in general and my ministry in particular would have been severely diminished.

So:

Who do you thank God for as a sister or brother in Christ?

Pray for Christians in the Eastern Orthodox tradition.

Prayer

> Lord God,
> whose servants Basil and Gregory
> proclaimed the mystery of your Word made flesh,
> to build up your church in wisdom and strength:
> grant that we may rejoice in His presence among us,
> and so be brought with them to know
> the power of your unending love;
> through Jesus Christ your Son our Lord.
> Amen

January 3rd ~ Takashi Nagai and Leonard Wilson

Takashi Nagai was born in Japan on 3rd January 1908. Converting to Christianity and becoming a Catholic in 1934 he was made Dean of Radiology at the University of Nagasaki. On August 9th 1945 the atomic bomb exploded on that city and amongst the 80,000 persons who died was his wife. Despite severing his carotid artery he immediately applied himself to the medical needs of the other survivors. The effects of radiation left Nagai an invalid and after living as a contemplative in a small hut near the ruined Cathedral he died in 1951 at the age of 43.

John Leonard Wilson was born in 1897 in Gateshead and after serving in the Durham Light Infantry during the First World War, entered the ministry of The Church of England. He was ordained in Coventry and later served as a missionary in Cairo. On his return to England, after a curacy at St Margaret's  Durham and St John's Neville Cross, he went as Vicar in Gateshead and later to Roker in Sunderland. He was invited by Bishop Hall to take up the post of Dean at Hong Kong cathedral before becoming Bishop of Singapore in 1941. When Singapore was captured by the Japanese later that year Wilson was taken prisoner, tortured, severely beaten, starved and imprisoned in Changi jail. After the Japanese surrender in 1945 Wilson returned to England and after ministry in Manchester became Bishop of Birmingham in 1953. He died in 1970.

Reflection

At a human level both these men inspire me for neither refused to hold any bitterness towards their aggressors. At a deeper level they puzzle me for the reasons they give for their forbearance. Leonard Wilson for instance thought that the Japanese did what they did because they were conditioned by their training and because of their worship of the Emperor and were therefore not to blame. Takashi Nagai noting that Nagasaki was the centre of Japanese Catholicism encouraged Christians to give thanks that it was the chosen victim, offered as a burnt offering on the altar of sacrifice atoning for the sins of all the nations during World War 2. The theology in both cases - and particularly the latter – is I think dubious yet it led both men to work for the cause of international peace and reconciliation. I met Leonard Wilson once when he came to our home for a meal and I can remember still as a young boy thinking I was in the presence of both a great and humble man of God even though I knew little of his sufferings. Others said much the same about Takashi Nagai. Jesus said "It is by their fruits you shall know them" not by their theology and it is for these they are known and honoured.

So:

Are there Christians who both puzzle and inspire you?

In what ways has God surprised you recently?

Prayer

> Lord, we remember those who like Takashi Nagai and Leonard Wilson suffered when madness ruled the world, and evil dwelt on earth. Because of their words of forgiveness and reconciliation may we renew our fight against cruelty and injustice, prejudice, tyranny, and oppression. Let not the hope of men and women perish. Let not new clouds rain death upon the earth. Turn to yourself the hearts and wills of rulers and peoples, that a new world may arise where men and women live as friends in the bond of your peace. Through Jesus Christ our Lord.
> Amen
>
> Jim Cotter (adapted)

January 4th ~ Barnabas

Though not named among the twelve apostles, Barnabas emerges in the Acts of the Apostles as one of the most significant of their number. He sold his estate and gave the proceeds to the Church, and he introduced Paul to the leaders of the Church in Jerusalem. He was sent to Antioch to encourage the growing church there and after a disagreement with Paul over Mark he went to Cyprus and tradition has it that he was martyred there in the year 61.

Reflection

"Who do you most look forward to meeting in heaven?" someone asked me a while ago. Well apart from some of those special people I've mentioned in this book - "my" saints - and those I love who have gone before me in faith, I think Barnabas would be top of my list - although I suspect there might be a queue! But I would want to thank Barnabas for being an example of that most basic, undervalued yet precious gift of encouragement. It's basic because it costs so little - except perhaps of one's pride, it's undervalued because rarely is it appreciated the difference it can make to another person, it's precious because most of us - and not least preachers - are always more liable to feel that we are inadequate than to get above ourselves. Of course there are dangers with encouragement - it can be bland and cover up deficiencies which should be addressed or become a drug which requires a regular fix but at its best it can enable a church or an individual to thrive in their Christian service knowing that they are neither unappreciated nor forgotten but valued and cherished and not simply in heaven but on earth too. Such encouragement Barnabas demonstrated towards the Church in Antioch and Saul, and later Mark. In Antioch the believers were called Christians for the first time, Saul became Paul the Apostle to the Gentiles and Mark wrote the earliest Gospel. And all as a result of encouragement! If we can offer nothing else to Christ and His people this New Year let us at least offer that. Who knows it might change a life, a church or even the world!

So:

Who do you look forward to meeting in heaven? Why?

Who needs encouraging by you today?

Prayer

> Free us, Lord from a spirit of cynicism
> or the desire to condemn,
> And make us, like Barnabas,
> Generous in our judgements,
> Bold in trusting others,
> And loyal to our friends.
> Fill us with your Spirit of encouragement,
> That we may be a source of support and comfort
> To all in need; for your love's sake.
> Amen

Angela Ashwin

Jeremiah received his call to be a prophet in 625 BC. He lived and taught during the final years of the southern kingdom of Judah and after the destruction of Jerusalem in 587 continued to work among the small remnant of people who were not deported to Babylon before finally going with them to Egypt. Like many of the other prophets his message was directed against those who believed that nothing could happen to Judah so long as the rituals of religion were observed, reminding them that true faithfulness to God must be reflected in mercy and justice. His warnings of impending judgement went unheeded and for much of his ministry he was ridiculed and persecuted and lived in fear of his life. Nevertheless after the destruction and exile (and also like many of the prophets who came before and after him) he spoke of hope and of a new beginning. For him, this was characterised in the Covenant which God had made with his people. No longer would the law be written on tablets of stone but upon their minds and hearts. They would know Him, and He would be their God and they His people forgiving their wickedness and remembering their sin no more.

Reflection

I suppose during my life-time I have attended well over one hundred Covenant Services with the saints of God in many and varied places. A few were memorable but most have faded from my mind. Sometimes the hymns, sermon and conduct of the service have added to the significance of the occasion but not always! And I am aware too that although the words of the Covenant Prayer have often left a deep impression on my mind I have realised occasionally that I have just been going through the motions. But it dawned on me at yesterday's Covenant Service what Jeremiah meant about tablets of stone. That it is not the form of words or merely the saying of them that is important, nor even whether I am in the right frame of mind or mood. These are external things. What is important is what is on God's heart and mind. He has not made a contract but a Covenant with me and in His heart is unconditional love. He has written that on my heart too that I may know and love and serve Him not out of fear but in joyful obedience and deep gratitude. Let it be so!

So:

What does the Covenant service mean to you?

Do you live by law or grace?

Prayer

> Eternal God,
> in your faithful and enduring love
> you call us to share in your gracious covenant in Jesus Christ.
> In obedience we hear and accept your commands;
> in love we seek to do your perfect will;
> with joy we offer ourselves anew to you.
> We are no longer our own but yours.
> Amen

January 6th ~ The Epiphany

The subtitle of this, one of the principal feasts of the Church is 'The Manifestation of Christ to the Gentiles'. This emphasises that, from the moment of the Incarnation, the good news of Jesus Christ is for all: Jew and Gentile, the wise and the simple, male and female. Nothing in the Greek text of the gospels indicates that the Magi were all male and even the number three and making them Kings is a much later non-scriptural tradition.

Reflection

Just before Christmas I visited Cologne for a day – or at least for half a day as the flight was delayed! I'd always wanted to go there although struggle to give a reason, but a combination of cheap flights, Christmas markets and a sabbatical suggested this was an opportune time! The Cathedral is magnificent, one of the largest in Europe, but until I arrived I hadn't realised that in the Middle Ages Cologne was a major place of pilgrimage for in 1164 the supposed bones of the "Three Magi" were transferred from Milan to Cologne and placed in a shrine which is still visited by thousands today.

My stay in Cologne was short like many who spent time in the Cathedral. And there is no indication in Matthew's Gospel that The Magi who came to see the infant Jesus in Bethlehem stayed over long. Yet their long journey and their short stay were life-changing and it brought them to their knees in worship and in presenting their gifts. And as I looked at their shrine in Cologne Cathedral I remembered and gave thanks for the Epiphany message that I and all who are pilgrims, fellow travellers, sight-seers, curious or simply passers-by are welcomed and invited to come and worship also and to offer our gifts, knowing they will not be turned away.

So:

Where is your faith-journey taking you this year?

What gifts are you bringing to the Christ-child?

Prayer

Jesus,
we offer you the gold of our desire to love,
even though our hearts are often cold;
we offer you the incense of our longing to pray,
although our spirits can be luke-warm;
we offer you the myrrh of our frustrations and troubles,
even when self-pity and bitterness creep in.
Receive and make good our gifts
out of your great love for us,
and grant that we, like the wise men,
may find some kneeling-space at Bethlehem.
Amen

Angela Ashwin

James, often called 'the Great', was a Galilean fisherman who, with his brother John, was one of the first apostles called by Jesus to follow Him. The two brothers were with Jesus at His Transfiguration and with Him again in the garden of Gethsemane. They annoyed the other followers of Jesus by asking to sit one on His left and the other on His right when He came into His glory and they were present for the appearances of Christ after the resurrection. James was put to death by the sword around the year 44 on the order of Herod Agrippa, who hoped in vain that he could stem the flow of those hearing the good news and becoming followers in the Way.

Reflection

The longest pilgrimage I have undertaken is to Santiago de Compostela and I only walked the final eighth of that, some 70 miles! The Camino, as it's called, is now the most well known and well used of all the Christian pilgrimage routes in the world although is travelled of course by those of all faiths and none and for a whole variety of reasons. Originally however, pilgrims made the journey to Santiago to honour St James - hence the scallop shell worn by pilgrims which is his symbol.

In the Cathedral of Santiago de Compostela is found a statue of St James as well as his relics and these are embraced no doubt as much out of relief and thankfulness at finishing the journey as anything else! But there is also a solid silver incense burner which weights a quarter of a ton and takes eight men to lift. As I saw it swinging over the altar during Mass I remembered that it had both a secular and sacred purpose. Practically it was there to mask the stale and sweaty smell of pilgrims who had walked hundreds of miles without a change of clothes or perhaps even a wash. But its deeper meaning was to remind pilgrims that all their thoughts, conversations, aspirations and prayers during their pilgrimage were lived out in the presence of God and now offered to Him to be cleansed, purified and blest. Incense was of course one of the gifts the Wise Men brought and whether we like its use in worship or not its symbolism is still the same, reminding us that in Christ sacred and secular are brought together and that all life may be offered to Him as a prayer.

So:

Is your life a prayer?

What pilgrimage do you need to make – even in your own home?

Prayer

> *Fix thou our steps, O Lord, that we stagger not at the uneven motions of the world, but steadily go on to our glorious home; neither censuring our journey by the weather we meet with, nor turning out of the way for anything that befalls us. The winds are often rough, and our own weight presses us downwards. Reach forth, O Lord, thy hand, thy saving hand, and speedily deliver us.*
>
> *Teach us, O Lord, to use this transitory life as pilgrims returning to their beloved home; that we may take what our journey requires and not think of settling in a foreign country.*
> *Amen*
>
> *John Wesley*

January 8th ~ Jim Elliot

Jim Elliot was born in 1927 in Portland, Oregon and brought up in a Christian family from which he found it natural both to hear the call to follow Christ and to serve on the mission field. After appropriate training he sailed to Ecuador in 1952 and worked for three years among the Quichua Indians. Learning of a small settlement of Huaorani Indians in a remote part of the Amazon jungle unreached by the Gospel and feared for their tenacity in defending their territory against all outsiders, Elliot and his four companions determined to make contact with them. After an initial peaceful contact all five were speared to death on this day in 1956. His wife Elisabeth stayed in Ecuador and subsequently worked among the Huaorani, leading many of them to faith.

Reflection

Whilst Jim Elliot's life and subsequent martyrdom have inspired many to hear the call to missionary service, his and Elisabeth's story has always personally challenged me to reflect on what it means to take risks for the Gospel's sake. To go to the Huaorani Indians in the first place was risk enough but to return knowing the likely consequences defies the imagination. Yet both lived by the words that Jim Elliot recorded in his diary the night before he died:- "He is no fool who gives what he cannot keep to gain what he cannot lose". So when I am tempted to "play it safe", maintain the status quo and neither rock the boat or stick my neck out and when individuals or churches are in danger of reacting in the same way I remember the risky living of Jim and Elisabeth Elliot in following a God of risks and ask for strength for myself and others to follow in their footsteps.

So:

When did you last take risks for the Gospel's sake?

What risks is God asking of you today?

Prayer

The words of this hymn formed the basis for the title of Jim and Elisabeth Elliot's biography: 'Through Gates Of Splendour'

We rest on Thee, our Shield and our Defender!
We go not forth alone against the foe;
Strong in Thy strength, safe in Thy keeping tender,
We rest on Thee, and in Thy Name we go.

We go in faith, our own great weakness feeling,
And needing more each day Thy grace to know:
Yet from our hearts a song of triumph pealing,
"We rest on Thee, and in Thy Name we go."

We rest on Thee, our Shield and our Defender!
Thine is the battle, Thine shall be the praise;
When passing through the gates of pearly splendour,
Victors, we rest with Thee, through endless days.

Edith G Cherry

January 9th ~ C.T. Studd and David Sheppard

Charles Thomas Studd was born in 1860. A talented athlete by the age of sixteen he was captain of cricket at Eton College and at Cambridge and was a member of the England Team that regained The Ashes in Australia in 1883. Through the influence of Moody and Sankey and as part of the "Cambridge Seven" - young graduates of wealth and privilege who renounced their promising careers - Studd gave up playing cricket and to the astonishment of colleagues, press and public went as a missionary to China. After his twenty-fifth birthday he gave away 9/10th of his inheritance to a variety of Christian Societies. Later he served in India and the Belgian Congo where he died in 1931 but not before he had established World Evangelisation Crusade (WEC) which today has some 1700 missionaries serving in more than 70 countries.

David Sheppard was born in 1929 and came to faith whilst a student in Cambridge. An accomplished cricketer, David Sheppard played 22 tests for England and captained his country twice but retired early from the game to pursue his vocation. After training for the Anglican ministry he worked at the Mayflower Family Centre in Canning Town before becoming Bishop of Woolwich in 1969 and Bishop of Liverpool in 1975, the youngest diocesan

bishop in England. A strong opponent of apartheid, an ecumenical enthusiast and with a passion for the poor and underprivileged he became Lord Sheppard of Liverpool in 1998. He died in 2005.

Reflection

I love sport - and cricket (in many ways even more than football) is a passion of mine, but the stories of C.T. Studd and David Sheppard are a sharp reminder of what is really important. It was after all David Sheppard who was the catalyst for my coming to faith. I had gone to hear him preach for he was a hero of mine and I was delighted when he used a cricketing illustration but it was only to reinforce his message about sin and God's way of salvation and that night I went forward to confess the first and receive the second. And although there have been many strands to the outworking of my call to the ministry C.T. Studd's words have been among them:- "If Christ be God and died for me, then no sacrifice can be too great for me to make for Him". So I can vividly recall an occasion when I had to make a stark choice between faith and football and his words provided the inspiration to make the right decision. I still love sport and am glad to be involved in it but I know now that it's not the be all and end all of life. C.T. Studd and David Sheppard remind me of what is of eternal significance and I thank God for them again today.

So:

What is of eternal significance to you?

Pray for Sports Chaplains who seek to minister to the here and now but point to the there and then.

Prayer

> In our joys and in our sorrows,
> days of toil and hours of ease,
> still he calls, in cares and pleasures:
> 'Christian, love me more than these.'
> Jesus calls us! By your mercies,
> Saviour, may we hear your call,
> give our hearts to your obedience,
> serve and love you best of all.
> Cecil Frances Alexander

January 10th ~ William Laud

William Laud was appointed Archbishop of Canterbury by his friend and ecclesiastical ally, King Charles in 1633. The aim of both Archbishop and Monarch was to counter the reforming Puritan movement which emphasised personal and ecclesial austerity as a means of sustaining conversion. Laud was a High Churchman who felt that the majesty of God should be reflected in the liturgy of the church and rigorously set about ensuring that its ministers should practise what he preached. His relentless approach left no room for variance of practice - but neither did the Puritans - and the latter had the upper hand in Parliament and eventually impeached him in 1640 and imprisoned him in the Tower of London. His friend the King did not - or could not - come to his assistance and he was beheaded on this day in 1645.

Reflection

I didn't know I had a love for liturgy until I served on The Faith and Order Committee. Having been brought up in a "high" Methodist Church where The Book of Offices was in regular use and as a student at theological college being subjected to all kinds of experimental liturgies in preparation for the then new Methodist Service Book, I longed for extempore prayer or "free worship" as it was often called. But when 25 years later I found myself a member of a small scrutiny group studying the texts for a new Worship Book, I came to realise how important words in worship were, especially when they are to be used on a regular basis and must stand the test of time. I had by that time experienced the way in which liturgy can come to life when it is used creatively and with enthusiasm and had also realised that whilst I still valued extempore or free worship it can be just as hide-bound or straight-jacketed as any liturgical form.

But in the end of course the only thing that really matters is that we offer our very best in worship to God. Despite his imperfections, shortcomings and misplaced zeal that is what William Laud and indeed The Puritans were seeking to do. It's a thousand pities that they could never recognise it in each other – and when we repeat their mistakes in our own day.

So:

What do you value about the different forms of worship you experience?

How informed are you as to why others worship as they do?

Prayer

> Gracious Father, we pray for your church.
> Fill it with your truth, and keep it in your peace.
> Where it is corrupt, purge it;
> Where it is in error, direct it;
> Where it is right, strengthen and confirm it;
> Where it needs help, provide for it;
> Where it is divided, heal it,
> And unite it in your love,
> Through Jesus Christ our Saviour.
> Amen

after William Laud

January 11th ~ Mary Slessor

Mary Slessor was born into a working-class, Presbyterian family in Aberdeen in 1848. As a child she was enthralled by stories of missions in Africa. For years she read diligently as she worked in the mills and eventually in 1875 she was accepted as a teacher for the mission in Calabar, Nigeria. Her fluency in the local language, physical resilience and lack of pretension endeared her to those to whom she ministered. She adopted unwanted children, particularly twins who would otherwise, according to local superstition, have been put to death. She was influential in organising trade and in settling disputes, contributing much to the development of the Okoyong people with whom she later settled. She died, still in Africa, on this day in 1915.

Reflection

It is a number of years since I handed out books at a Sunday School prizegiving but I do remember my own. We were given a list of six "inspiring" books to choose from but by the age of 12 the only one left that I hadn't read was the life of Mary Slessor so I grudgingly received that - and was captivated! Many years later one of the members of my youth fellowship also heard her life story and was captivated too - so much so that she followed in her footsteps to Nigeria working for the Leprosy Mission. It was a privilege to visit her there a while ago and to see all that God was doing through her as she worked in a way not dissimilar to that of Mary Slessor a century before.

The Primitive Methodists had a saying "God buries His workers but continues His work", and that was never more true than of Mary Slessor. It is 99 years ago today since she died but through the story of her life heard by two young people many years and many miles apart God inspired one and called another. God moves in a mysterious way but He performs wonders as He does. So Paul encourages us all:- "Be steadfast, immovable in your work for The Lord for you know that in the Lord your labour is not in vain" (1 Corinthians 15 v 58).

So:

How have you seen God's mysterious wonders worked out in your life?

What book has inspired you to live or act differently?

Prayer

For all the saints
Who went before us
Who have spoken to our hearts
And touched us with your fire,
We praise you, O God.
For all the saints
Who live beside us
Whose weaknesses and strengths
Are woven with our own,
We praise you, O God.
For all the saints
Who live beyond us
Who challenge us
To change the world with them,
We praise you, O God.
Amen

Janet Morley

January 12th ~ Aelred and Benedict Biscop

Aelred was born at Hexham in 1109. His father was a priest and he entered the Cistercian Order at Rievaulx in about 1133. He became Abbot of Revesby in 1143 and returned to Rievaulx four years later to become abbot and to spend the remainder of his life. He was profoundly influential through his spiritual writings, which he began at the request of Bernard of Clairvaux, the two having a similar approach to the spiritual life. Because of this Aelred was often called "The Bernard of the North". He died on this day at Rievaulx in 1167.

Benedict Biscop was born a Northumbrian nobleman in 628. He served at the court of King Oswiu of Northumbria until he joined Wilfrid of York on his pilgrimage to Rome to the tombs of the apostles. He made a second trip accompanied by the King's son and on his way home was clothed a monk at the Benedictine house of Lerins. It was on his third trip to Rome that he met and returned to England with Theodore, the newly-appointed Archbishop of Canterbury, who made him Abbot of St Augustine's in 669. Five years later, he was permitted to make his own foundation at Wearmouth which he built in the Roman style and endowed with a huge library. His own scholarship, and that promoted through the religious houses he founded, played a large part in the acceptance of the primacy of Roman over Celtic practice throughout northern England. Benedict Biscop died on this day in 689.

RefLection

Two more of my "local" Saints are remembered today (how many there were from the north-east!) and both have been a part of my pilgrimage walks - Aelred most recently when I visited Rievaulx on The Whitby Way and Benedict Biscop in 2007 when I walked with the then President of Conference Martyn Atkins from Holy Island to Monkwearmouth in the footsteps of the Northern Saints.

Saints are often thought of as holy men and women and in a sense that's true as long as we remember that in the New Testament particularly, holiness is far more to do with specialness than separation. So whilst both Aelred and Benedict Biscop lived as monks - separate to an extent from the world - it wasn't this that marked them out but rather that they were special people - the former renowned for the depth of his friendships and his love for God and the latter for his gentleness and grace. And such saintliness today - for us as well as for others - is still best expressed through such qualities as these.

So:

What are the special qualities in other Christians that attract you?

Is there something so special about your life that others are drawn to Christ?

Prayer

> O God, let me feel this world as thy love taking form,
> then my love will help it.
> Amen

Rabindranath Tagore

January 13th ~ George Fox

George Fox was born at Fenny Drayton in Leicestershire in 1624, the son of a weaver and was himself apprenticed to a shoe-maker. The 'Inner Light of the Living Christ' became his watchword in 1646 and he began to preach that the truth could only be found through the Inner Voice speaking directly to each soul. His society of 'The Friends of Truth' was formed at about this time, and many believers joined. Fox spent several spells in gaol because of his determination to preach where he would and what he willed. He had a charismatic personality combined with excellent organisational abilities, which proved a solid foundation for ensuring the continuance of his beliefs and practices. He died on this day in 1691.

Reflection

I learnt today how The Quakers got their name! Apparently it was coined after George Fox told a magistrate to "tremble before the Lord" and although intended as a term of abuse - like the word Methodist - the name stuck.

Quaking or trembling are not words we often use to describe our encounters with God - although a hymn often sung during the Epiphany season does speak of coming to God in "trembling and fearfulness". Perhaps it's because trembling (and fear) conjures up a picture of a tyrant towering over his subject who cowers before him quaking. Yet Jesus in his parables is very clear that God is precisely the opposite of that so to tremble in His presence is simply to recognise with awe and wonder a God who stoops down in love to hear our longings and receive our prayers. It was this possibility of direct communication with God – the Inner Light as he called it – that was George Fox's great contribution to a church which in the mid-seventeenth century had become so bound up in ritual and wrangling that it had forgotten to nurture a relationship with God or even consider it possible. The fact that he went to extremes to make his point in ways which we might consider unhelpful, or discarded the things which we find helpful, shouldn't blind us to the fact that we too need to hear again the call to intimacy with God which is at the heart of The Gospel.

So:

When did you last tremble before the Lord?

Is "The Inner Light" enough?

Prayer

> O Christ,
> Serene and tranquil light,
> Shine into the depth of my being,
> Come, and draw me to yourself.
> Free me from the chatter of my mind,
> And draw me through and beyond
> All words and symbols,
> Into the silence,
> That I may discover You,
> The unspoken Word,
> The pure light,
> Piercing and transforming the darkness
> That veils the ground of my being.
> Amen

Based on words by FC Happold

January 14th ~ Martin Niemoeller

Martin Niemoeller was born on this day in 1892. Decorated as a German U-Boat Commander during World War 1 he regarded the war's loss with a deep sense of betrayal and the Versailles Treaty as a humiliation. Following in his father's footsteps as a Lutheran pastor, Niemoeller was also an early supporter of National Socialism, believing in Hitler's promise to vindicate German honour. However he became increasingly uneasy with the ideology and extension of the Nazis and helped found the Confessing Church which attracted over 2000 pastors including Karl Barth and Dietrich Bonhoeffer. Within a few years the Confessing Church was supressed, its members either having capitulated or been imprisoned, exiled or murdered. Niemoeller was arrested in 1937 – church bells throughout the country being rung in protest - and although found guilty of "rebellion against the state" the judges refused to commit this war hero to prison. Hitler dismissed them and insisted that Niemoeller be sent to Sachenhausen Concentration Camp as his personal prisoner. He was later sent to Dachau where he remained until the end of the war. Parting company with fellow Germans who refused to own any responsibility for Nazi atrocities, he acknowledged his share in what he saw as their collective guilt particularly in his failure to speak out on behalf of the Jews. Guided by the principle "What would Jesus do?" later to be taken up by countless millions of Christians throughout the world, Niemoeller became a prominent figure in the pacifist movement. He died peacefully in 1984 at the age of 92.

Reflection

Collective guilt is I think a difficult concept to grasp. My own sins are as the psalmist put it "ever before me" and maybe I can identify with the sins of the church, particularly a local one. But to acknowledge guilt towards those I have never met or a part of the world I have never visited is much harder. Yet if it is true that "no one is an island" and that when I drop a pebble in the sea the mighty ocean moves then my actions and attitudes may have far more reaching consequences for good or ill than I realise. So when greed, selfishness, pride and indifference are found in me then they also contribute to such things in the world and I cannot escape responsibility. As Niemoeller reminds us it is only when we acknowledge our sins and confess our guilt that there is forgiveness and the possibility of new beginnings.

So:

What decisions do you make that affect others?

"What would Jesus do?" Is that a good guiding principle to live by?

Prayer

The sins of the world, such dreadful sins, not just the personal sins but the solidarity of sin greater than the total of individual sins.

O Lamb of God, forgive my sins, cleanse my heart, disarm my will and let me fight armed with thy truth, righteousness and love with the cross of love incised upon my heart, O Lamb of God.

Amen

George Appleton - adapted

January 15th ~ Donald English

Donald English was born in Consett, County Durham in 1930. Studying at Leicester University during which he had football trials with Leicester City he spent three years as travelling secretary for the Inter-Varsity Fellowship before candidating for the Methodist Ministry. After training he became Assistant Tutor at Headingley, went as a mission partner to Nigeria and served at Cullercoats before becoming tutor in practical theology and Methodism first in Manchester and then in Bristol. In 1982 he became Secretary of the Methodist Home Mission Division and remained there until his retirement in 1995. As the only person to have served twice as President of the Methodist Conference (1978 and 1990) Donald English was also Chair of The World Methodist Council (1991-1996), Moderator of the Free Church Federal Council (1986) and founder of Conservative Evangelicals in Methodism (now Methodist Evangelicals Together). He was a regular contributor to Thought For The Day on Radio 4 and played a prominent role in political and social life for which he was awarded a CBE in 1996. He died in Oxford in 1998.

Reflection

Donald English was quite simply my Father in God. I first met him when he became tutor at Wesley College Bristol during my second year there and we immediately struck up a rapport, no doubt through a common interest in football! He encouraged me to join Conservative Evangelicals in Methodism so that I might become a thinking evangelical rather than a naive or narrow one and helped me build a framework for my faith in which "Christ holds all things together". (It was partly due to him that I used these words from

Paul's letter to the Colossians as the theme for my Presidential Address in 2011.) It was wonderful and strangely fitting therefore that he should be the Presiding Minister at my Ordination in 1978. When I was asked to follow him at Cullercoats he was thrilled - or so he said - and I was deeply moved when he came to preach for me a few months after his beloved wife's death and a few months before his own. I miss him still and think of him often - not least when I am writing sermons and a compelling phrase of his comes to mind or I hear him say when I've finished preparing:- "So what?" His influence upon me has been immeasurable and I give thanks to God for every remembrance of him and of his ministry which through his imprint on others continues to bless the church today.

So:

Who is your Father or Mother in God?

Who would you like to have a Godly and lasting influence on?

Prayer

The words of a hymn sung at Donald English's funeral

Now I have found the ground wherein
sure my soul's anchor may remain —
the wounds of Jesus, for my sin
before the world's foundation slain;
whose mercy shall unshaken stay,
when heaven and earth are fled away.
Fixed on this ground will I remain,
though my heart fail and flesh decay;
this anchor shall my soul sustain,
when earth's foundations melt away;
mercy's full power I then shall prove,
loved with an everlasting love.

Ich habe nun den Grund gefunden
by Johann Andreas Rothe (1688-1758)
translated by John Wesley (1703-1791)

January 16th ～ Julian of Norwich, Edith Cavell, Elizabeth Fry and Margery Kempe

In 1373 when she was thirty years old, a woman of Norwich, whose own name is unrecorded, experienced a series of sixteen visions, which revealed aspects of the love of God. She spent the next twenty years of her life pondering their meaning and recorded her conclusions in what became the first book written by a woman in English, The Revelations of Divine Love. She became an anchoress attached to the Church of St Julian in Norwich and it was by this name of Julian that she came to be known to later generations. She died around the year 1417.

Edith Cavell was born at Swardeston in Norfolk in 1865. After life as a governess she trained as a nurse, ending up working in Belgium in 1907. On the outbreak of the First World War, she became involved in caring for the wounded on both sides. She refused repatriation and then began smuggling British soldiers from Belgium into Holland. She was arrested, brought to trial, sentenced to death and executed by firing squad on 12 October 1915. She went to her death calmly, forgiving her executioners, convinced she had been doing her duty as a Christian.

Elizabeth Fry was born at Earlham in Norfolk in 1780. She was a minister in the Society of Friends and became a noted preacher. The appalling state of the prisons came to her notice and she devoted much of her time to the welfare of female prisoners in Newgate. She was a woman of a strong Christian and evangelistic impulse and this inspired all her work. She died in 1845.

Margery Kempe was born at Lynne in Norfolk in the late fourteenth century, a contemporary of Julian of Norwich. She received many visions, and also had conversations with the saints. She was much sought after as a visionary, was endlessly in trouble with the Church, and was more than once imprisoned. Following the messages in her visions, she undertook pilgrimages to many holy places, often setting out penniless. She was blessed with the gift of tears and developed a strong compassion for the sins of the world. She died towards the middle of the fifteenth century.

Reflection

Four for the price of one today – with the link that they were all born in Norfolk! However they also had in common that they were all visionaries, for each in quite different ways was given an insight into God's purposes for humanity and to what this "looking beyond" required of them in terms of prayer, pilgrimage, prison reform or patriotism – even though it resulted in hardship, misunderstanding, opposition and death. Perhaps we have been given visions too – even though we may not call them that – of how God sees the world or the church, of how they can yet be and of the part we can play to bring such change about. St Paul says that he was not disobedient to the heavenly vision. Nor must we be.

So:

What "visions" have you received recently? Which of these four saints impresses you most? Why is each important?

Prayer

Lord Jesus, I am not an eagle. All I have are the eyes and the heart of one. In spite of my littleness, I dare to gaze at the sun of love, and long to fly toward it. I want to imitate the eagles, but all I can do is flap my small wings. What shall I do? With cheerful confidence I shall stay gazing at the sun till I die. Nothing will frighten me, neither wind nor rain, and my heart is at peace.
Amen

Therese of Lisieux 1873-97

January 17th ~ Charles Gore

Born in 1835, Gore became one of the most influential of Anglican theologians. He helped reconcile the church to some aspects of Biblical criticism and scientific discovery, yet was Catholic in his interpretation of the faith and sacraments. He was also concerned to bring Catholic principles to bear on social problems. As an Oxford don and then as a Canon of Westminster, he was renowned for his preaching. In the 1890's he was the founder and first leader of the Community of the Resurrection, which in later years settled at Mirfield in Yorkshire. From 1902 he was successively Bishop of Worcester, Birmingham and Oxford. He was much mourned at his death on this day in 1932.

Reflection

My memories of Charles Gore are bitter sweet. When after playing Queens College Birmingham at football one of their students presented me with a picture to take back to Wesley College Bristol I didn't think much about it even if the tradition was to "steal" something rather than be given it! What I hadn't realised however was that this was a priceless portrait of Charles Gore - the founder of Queens College - and that to hang it in the toilets at Wesley College was not the wisest thing to do! After a frantic conversation between both principals I was ordered to immediately return it to Birmingham which I did - in the middle of the night!

My own memories of theological education are bitter sweet too. When I was in college I couldn't wait to get stared in Circuit, felt that I was being given information rather than being taught how to learn, couldn't relate the theoretical to the practical and concurred with a former student that what he had learned could be written on the back of a postage stamp! In looking back however I realise how much I did owe to my four years in Bristol. Lifelong friendships, the imparting of wisdom as well as knowledge, "tools for ministry" which I still use today and the time to talk things through, tease things out and have assumptions challenged corrected or strengthened was precious and I am very grateful.

Now things have come full circle and as Chair of The Ministries Committee I have among other things the formation of ministers as part of my brief not least at Queens College! Perhaps some of the lessons I learnt, the mistakes I made and the things that could have been done differently will stand me in good stead. At the very least it is yet another example of God's amazing sense of humour!

So:

Are you still a learner in the school of Christ?

How are you supporting those in ministry both lay and ordained?

Prayer

> *On the peoples of the world and the leaders of the nations,*
> *On your holy Church throughout the world,*
> *On all whom you have called to be ordained,*
> *On all whom they serve in their ministry,*
> *On their families and friends and all who have helped and encouraged them,*
> *gracious God,*
> *pour out your Spirit.*
> *Amen*
>
> From the Methodist Ordination Service

January 18th ~ Week of prayer for Christian Unity

The week of prayer for Christian Unity was first observed in the 1890's by Roman Catholics and Anglicans in the period between the feasts of Ascension Day and Pentecost - although separately! It was not until 1908 that the dates were changed to coincide with the Confession of Peter (January 18th) and the Conversion of Paul (January 25th) and was only universally recognised and participated in during the 1930's, whilst pulpit exchanges, special services, home and prayer groups across the denominations only became commonplace after the second Vatican Council (1964) when Catholics were both permitted and encouraged to meet together with other Christians to mark this special week. Ironically this meant that in some places their inclusion led others to opt out!

Reflection

I guess the watershed for The Week of Prayer for Christian Unity was the 1960's. Catholics were now full participants, the Anglican/Methodist Union talks were in full swing and Presbyterians and Congregationalists were to achieve that which Methodists and Anglicans failed to do in 1972. So as a teenager I remember the Week of Prayer as a highlight in the local churches with large congregations, major events, joint study groups and the icing on the cake being a service in the Catholic Church! Such days are rarely found now. Some describe the period we are now passing through as a winter time for ecumenism (although others see signs of spring) but dashed hopes and dreams, a politeness that has avoided real engagement and a decline in church attendance leading to apathy or a battening down of the hatches has meant that if the Week of Prayer is observed at all it tends to be for the sake of ticking boxes more than out of real conviction. Whilst prayers may be offered in the intercessions, special services are often now only attended by enthusiasts and as an "add on" rather than important in their own right. Whilst I am deeply saddened by this I am glad that at least the week is still marked and of course rejoice at the huge steps forward that have been made ecumenically in terms of closer understanding and better ways of working than could have been imagined 50 years ago. In the end this should always matter more than what we do on a particular week in the year. But my prayer is that new opportunities may yet open up to deepen that unity which is both a gift and a goal not simply for its own sake but so that as Jesus prayed "the world might believe". In the meantime I continue to thank God for his saints in other Christian traditions who have deepened my faith, challenged my pre-conceptions, shared their treasures and drawn me closer to Jesus the head of the whole body.

So:

What have you received from other Christians?

How can you further the unity for which Christ prayed?

Prayer

Lord God, we thank you for calling us into the company of those who trust in Christ and seek to obey His will. May your Spirit guide and strengthen us in mission and service to your world for we are strangers no longer but pilgrims together on the way to your Kingdom. Amen

Churches Together in Britain and Ireland

January 19th ~ Wulfstan

Born in about the year 1009, Wulfstan's first twenty-five years after his ordination were spent in the monastery at Worcester. Against his will he was elected Bishop of Worcester in 1062 but went on to prove an able administrator and pastor. He carefully and gently nurtured both church and state through the transition from Saxon to Norman rule. He died at Worcester on this day in the year 1095.

Reflection

I "collect" cathedrals almost as much as football grounds so I was delighted to have the opportunity to visit Worcester in the autumn– a cathedral I must have visited fifty or so years ago but of which I have no recollection. The mid-day Eucharist was celebrated by a retired priest who looked about as old as Wulfstan himself and who stumbled through the service but I reflected that without him and no doubt others the worship of God in that place would have been diminished. As a "do-er" near retirement I am well aware that I will need those around me who will say "enough is enough", but I am also conscious that it is not simply in cathedrals but in churches and chapels across the land that retired clergy "keep the show on the road" – sometimes with little acknowledgement or appreciation. So today I thank God for all who see retirement as a comma rather than a full stop in their Christian service, as an opening up rather than a closing down and who willingly share their God-given gifts, experience and wisdom with others. The Bible is full of those who came into their own long after "retirement" and the psalmist speaks of those who still bear fruit even in old age. I hope the same can be said of me.

So:

Who in their old age has blessed you?

In what holy place have you encountered God?

Prayer

> *Lord God,*
> *Who raised up Wulfstan to be a bishop among your people*
> *and a leader of your church:*
> *Help us, after his example,*
> *to live simply,*
> *to work diligently*
> *and to make your kingdom known;*
> *through Jesus Christ your Son our Lord,*
> *Who is alive and reigns with you,*
> *In the unity of the Holy Spirit,*
> *One God, now and for ever.*
> *Amen*

January 20th ~ Gordon Wilson

Gordon Wilson was born in County Leitrim in the Irish Free State in September 1927 but moved across the border to Enniskillen, County Fermanagh at an early age. A life-long Methodist, he worked in his draper's shop only coming to prominence when on 8th November 1987 a bomb planted by the Provisional IRA at the town's Cenotaph during the Remembrance Day Service killed 11 people including his daughter Marie. In an emotional television interview he gave only hours after the bombing he said: "I bear no ill will, I bear no grudge" and later said that he was praying for the perpetrators of the outrage. Whereas many IRA attacks in Northern Ireland resulted in reprisals by loyalists, Wilson's call for forgiveness and reconciliation came to be known as The Spirit of Enniskillen. The BBC would later describe the bombing and Gordon Wilson's response to it as a turning point in the troubles. In 1993 Gordon Wilson was invited to become a member of the Upper House in The Irish Republic and through his speeches there, his regular meetings with Sinn Fein (and on one occasion with the Provisional IRA) his speaking engagements and broadcasts and his Trust designed to help young people build bridges across the communities, Gordon Wilson never ceased to espouse the cause of forgiveness, reconciliation and peace despite some on both sides who dismissed him as naive, foolish or of "selling out". After suffering a second bereavement in his son Peter's death, Gordon Wilson died of a heart attack in 1995 at the age of 67.

Reflection

I never met Gordon Wilson but one of the highlights of my year as

President was to talk to his wife Joan at Enniskillen Methodist church during the Irish Conference. Rarely have I seen such transparent faith and goodness shine in another's face but on reading Gordon Wilson's biography came to realise that such Christ-likeness had not come easily to either of them but had been ground in the mill of suffering and pain and a sense of rejection and failure. Yet like Gordon - and like her Lord - Joan has gone on steadfastly in the ways of peace even if it has often meant walking the way of the cross too. And although Easter in its entirety hasn't yet come to Northern Ireland signs of resurrection and hope abound not least as the result of one man who in the words of the old hymn decided to "trust in God and do the right".

So:

In whom do you see Christ-likeness?

How is Christ-likeness being formed in you?

Prayer

> As we gaze on your kingly brightness
> so our faces display your likeness,
> ever changing from glory to glory:
> mirrored here, may our lives tell your story –
> shine on me, shine on me.
>
> Shine, Jesus, shine,
> fill this land with the Father's glory;
> blaze, Spirit, blaze,
> set our hearts on fire.
> Flow, river, flow,
> flood the nations with grace and mercy;
> send forth your word,
> Lord, and let there be light!
>
> Amen

Graham Kendrick

The reason Agnes is one of the most well-known and widely regarded of the early Roman martyrs is perhaps because of the expression of mature resilience and sheer bravery in a thirteen year old girl. Agnes is reputed to have refused an arranged marriage because of her total dedication to Christ and stated that she preferred even death of the body to the death of her consecrated virginity. The growing veneration for the state of consecrated virginity at this time, combined with the last, major Roman persecution under the emperor Diocletian, climaxing in the shedding of an innocent child's blood willingly for Christ, placed her at the forefront of veneration almost from the moment the persecution ended. She is believed to have died in the year 304 and her feast has ever since been celebrated on this day.

Reflection

Agnes has been heralded as a champion of both women and children – aged thirteen she could be described as either or both.

As a women she refused to be simply identified in terms of her sexuality for the God she worshipped set an altogether different value on her body, her identity and her human worth. Espoused to God she chose to be counter-cultural even if it cost her her life. As a child she exemplified the words of Jesus that unless we became as children we shall never enter the Kingdom of Heaven. Simplicity, trust and a sense of wonder must have been partly at least what Jesus had in mind when he used this analogy – childlikeness rather than childishness or seeking to return to some innocent state. Although Ambrose's remark that "Agnes went to her place of execution more cheerfully than others to their wedding" may be somewhat wide of the mark, nevertheless in her living and dying Agnes never lost her trust in the God who had created her, redeemed her and would welcome her home. Whether woman, child or neither, each of us is invited to find our true identity and our lasting security in that same God whom Agnes knew and loved over seventeen hundred years ago.

So:

What is your true identity?

Are women and children rightly valued in our society today?

Prayer

> Eternal God, Shepherd of your sheep,
> Whose child Agnes was strengthened to bear witness
> in her living and her dying
> to the true love of her Redeemer:
> grant us the power to understand, with all your saints,
> what is the breadth and length and height and depth
> and to know the love that surpasses knowledge,
> even Jesus Christ your Son our Lord,
> who is alive and reigns with you,
> in the unity of the Holy Spirit,
> one God, now and for ever.
> Amen

January 22nd ~ Maximilian Kolbe

Maximilian Kolbe was born at Zdunska Wola near Lodz in Poland in 1894. His parents were Franciscan Tertiaries and, beginning his training for ordination in 1907, Maximilian joined the Franciscan noviciate in 1910. After suffering a severe illness he resolved to publish a magazine for Christian readers and this soon gained a huge circulation. After the Nazi invasion of Poland, Maximilian was arrested as an 'intellectual' and taken to Auschwitz in May 1941. There he continued his priestly ministry, secretly celebrating the Eucharist. When after an escape a prisoner was chosen to forfeit his life as an example, Maximilian stepped forward to take his place and be put to death.

Reflection

When I began these reflections on saints I hadn't realised how often cells of one kind or another would feature but I have already mentioned Nelson Mandela, Thomas Merton, John of the Cross, Teresa of Avila, Hilda of Whitby, Martin Niemoeller and Julian of Norwich in this regard and Cuthbert, John Bunyan and Terry Waite are still to come! Some of these chose to live there for spiritual reasons, others were imprisoned against their will but although Maximilian Kolbe spent only fifteen days in his cell this was altogether different. Visiting Auschwitz a number of years ago moved and challenged me deeply at a number of levels. The first was the sudden realisation that these events took place only eleven years before I was born and when my eldest brother was already two so I was not visiting a museum recording ancient history but a place that was in some ways part of my own story. The second was being unable to imagine how Maximilian Kolbe did what he did and how much the grace of God must have been active in him at that moment. Third, that in common with all the "saints in cells", although in very different circumstances, Kolbe found in darkness and isolation the light and presence of Christ as perhaps never before. Finally that it is in the offering of himself that Maximilian is best remembered not least by the man whose place he took and who was present when Pope John Paul II canonised Kolbe in 1982. So in some ways Maximilian Kolbe seems very close to this present time, in another very distant, yet he reminds us that we are best remembered when we lay down our lives for others and closest to God when we offer Him our moments of darkness or loneliness, trusting Him for what is to come, even though it may lead through the valley of the shadow of death. It is in this that the Father is glorified.

So:

What have you learned about God when you have been in "a cell"?

What are your experiences of evil? How did you respond?

Prayer

> *Giver of Life,*
> *We wait with you to bear your hope to earth's darkest places:*
> *We wait at the places where darkness*
> *Is deeper than the deepest pain.*
> *Where love is denied: let forgiveness break through.*
> *Where justice is destroyed: let righteousness rule.*
> *Where hope is crucified: let faith persist.*
> *Where peace is fragile: let grace be strong.*
> *Where truth is sought: let the quest continue.*
> *Giver of life we wait and watch and pray with you.*
> *Amen*
>
> *Robin Green (adapted)*

Little is known of Hosea's background except that he was a contemporary of Isaiah, Amos and Micah and therefore prophesied in 8th century B.C. His message is an acted parable for after his wife Gomer proves unfaithful he takes her back as his own. In the same way, despite Israel's unfaithfulness, Hosea declares that God will not abandon her and calls for her to repent and seek God's mercy and forgiveness, confident in His overflowing love.

Reflection

I studied the minor prophets at 'A-level' and they make for grim reading! Hosea seems to be the exception for although he also speaks about impending judgement it is set in the context of God's unfailing love. Whether it was in Hosea's or God's mind for Gomer to be taken back it was still an incredibly difficult thing to do - akin to Joseph taking Mary to be his wife - and likely to have led to as much ridicule and incomprehension. But in so doing Hosea speaks to us of what it truly means to forgive those who wrong us but also of a God who despite the wilfulness and waywardness of the church as unfaithful whore or neglectful bride will never abandon her for He loves her with an everlasting love. But such grace should not be taken cheaply for it comes at great cost. Thus unwittingly or otherwise Hosea points us towards Calvary.

So:

How unconditional is your forgiveness?

Do you ever treat grace cheaply?

Prayer

Wilt thou forgive that sin where I begun,
Which was my sin, though it were done before?
Wilt thou forgive that sin, through which I run,
And do run still: though still I do deplore?
When thou hast done, thou hast not done,
For I have more.

Wilt thou forgive that sin by which I have won
Others to sin, and made my sin their door?
Wilt thou forgive that sin which I did shun
A year or two; but wallowed in a score?
When thou hast done, thou hast not done,
For I have more.

I have a sin of fear, that when I've spun
My last thread, I shall perish on the shore;
Swear by thyself that at my death thy son
Shall shine - as He shines now, and heretofore;
And having done that, thou hast done,
I fear no more.

John Donne

January 24th ~ Francis de Sales

Francis de Sales was born in 1567 in the castle at Sales in Savoy. He was educated in Paris and Padua, first as a legal advocate and then as a priest. In 1599 he was appointed Bishop-Coadjutor of Geneva and moved to Annecy from where he administered the diocese when he became the diocesan in 1602. In his preaching and writings, particularly his book 'Introduction to the Devout Life,' Francis concentrated in putting prayer and meditation within reach of all Christians. He died at Lyons in December 1622 and his body was translated to Annecy on this day in 1623.

Reflection

As the Week of Prayer for Christian Unity draws towards its close it's fitting that today the Church should remember Francis de Sales for he understood that the Church's life had to be founded on love not law, ("The measure of love is to love without measure") that the church's task is to live out everyday holiness and not simply practise religious observance ("The practice of devotion has to be adapted to the strength, life-situation and duties of each individual") and that the church's witness is first and foremost to a God of forgiveness and grace not condemnation and rejection ("Alas my poor heart, here we are, fallen into the pit we were so firmly resolved to avoid! Well we must get up again and leave it forever") So for Francis de Sales the truth of Christianity was always more than a set of propositions that you accepted or rejected. This led to disunity and discord. Rather it was truth worked out through truly living the way of Christ. We would do well to take Francis de Sales God-given insights to heart today. It would save us from so many disappointments and cul-de-sacs on the road to Christian unity and focus us both on what we already have in common and what we should be praying might be seen in greater measure among us.

So:

What do you think are the greatest barriers to Christian unity?

What do you have in common with other Christians?

Prayer

If only I possessed the grace, good Jesus, to be utterly at one with you! Amidst all the variety of worldly things around me, Lord, the only thing I crave is unity with you. You are all my soul needs. Unite, dear friend of my heart, this unique little soul of mine to your perfect goodness. You are all mine; when shall I be yours? Lord Jesus, my beloved, be the magnet of my heart; clasp, press, unite me for ever to your sacred heart. You have made me for yourself; make me one with you. Absorb this tiny drop of life into the ocean of goodness whence it came. Amen

Francis de Sales

January 25th ~ The Conversion of Paul

The conversion of the anti-Christian zealot, Saul, to the apostle of Christ, Paul, is clearly related in the Acts of the Apostles, but it has to be remembered that this was only a beginning: Saul took some time to become Paul and some time to begin to understand that his call to preach - to Jew and to Gentile - the saving power of Jesus, the son of God, was something that was a whole life's journey for him.

Reflection

Conversion occurs for some people at a point in time but is for all people a process that takes a life-time. It is fashionable in some circles to dismiss sudden conversions and to devalue the altar call - perhaps a reaction to those who fell by the wayside even before they had begun, or to over-emotional appeals. But some people do come to faith in an instant and it would be wise not to deny such an opportunity simply because it is not the way everyone comes.

Nevertheless Augustine was surely right when he declared: "I am saved. I am being saved, I will be saved", and although Paul's conversion is often spoken of as being instantaneous, his religious training and Stephen's testimony as he was being stoned to death must have had some part to play even if only that it made him ask the right questions. But it is equally true that God still had more "converting" to do in Paul's life as his reference to doing the things that he hates and not doing the things he wants to do (Romans 7) and not yet having attained the prize (Philippians 3) bears out. Nevertheless he could speak of being changed from glory into glory (2 Corinthians 3) and the assurance of knowing that nothing in life or death could separate him from God's love (Romans 8).

So conversion is both an experience to be treasured and a goal to be sought, guarding us against anxiety on one hand and presumption on the other. Paul's road to Damascus may not be the road on which we all travel but we must surely travel one of our own.

So:

What does conversion mean to you?

How is your "journey of conversion" working out?

Prayer

O Lord our God, we thank you for your amazing grace in calling Saul of Tarsus, the enemy and persecutor of the Church, to be Christ's dedicated servant and apostle, and to bear witness to him among the nations.

As today we recall his conversion we pray that we may know the same grace in our own lives, and like him may never be ashamed of the gospel.

We ask it in the name of Him who came into the world to save sinners, Jesus Christ our Lord.

Amen

Frank Colquhoun

January 26th ~ Timothy and Titus

On the day following the Conversion of St Paul, the church remembers two of his companions, 'partners and fellow-workers in God's service'. Timothy, we are told had a Jewish mother and a Greek father, whilst Titus was wholly Greek. It was because of Titus that Paul stood out against compulsory circumcision but to avoid suspicion from other Jews, Timothy was circumcised. They are honoured in the Church for their devotión and faithfulness to the gospel.

Reflection

We can't be entirely sure how old Timothy and Titus were when at various times they accompanied Paul on his missionary journeys but clearly they were younger than he both in age and Christian experience. So whilst Timothy and Titus provided companionship for Paul he in turn taught, mentored, supported, prayed and encouraged them as his "children in the faith".

When I look back over my life and ministry I think that I shall be most thankful if I have been in any sense what Paul was to Timothy and Titus. It has been such a joy to have played a part in the journey of some eighteen people towards ordination or full-time Christian service (and indirectly many more through Candidates, Oversight and Probationers Committees) and to see what God is doing through them today. I have presided, assisted or preached at many of their Ordinations and these have been wonderful occasions. Every person has a special place in my heart and prayers. And perhaps there are others too whom I have helped in their following of Jesus in some way. But it has not been one way traffic for in their various ways each has been a companion to me. Some have worked alongside me, others have shared my own spiritual journey and still others have excited and challenged me by their growing faith, the depth of their call and their difficult questions! But all have been faithful friends and showed care and concern for me in so many ways. Paul was as thankful for Timothy and Titus as they were for him and today I am so thankful for my "children in the faith" and for my companions "on the road".

So:

Who are your companions in faith?

Who are you mentoring in Christian discipleship?

Prayer

> *Heavenly Father,*
> *who sent your apostle Paul to preach the gospel,*
> *and gave him Timothy and Titus*
> *to be his companions in faith:*
> *grant that our fellowship in the Holy Spirit*
> *may bear witness to the name of Jesus,*
> *who is alive and reigns with you,*
> *in the unity of the Holy Spirit,*
> *one God, now and for ever.*
> *Amen*

January 27th ~ George Herbert

Born in 1593, George Herbert went up to Cambridge in 1614, eventually becoming a fellow of Trinity College. At the age of twenty-five he became Public Orator in the University and then a Member of Parliament, apparently destined for a life at court. To everyone's surprise he decided to be ordained and after spending a time with his friend Nicholas Ferrar at Little Gidding, he was made deacon in 1626. He married in 1629, was priested in 1630 and given the care of souls of the parish of Bemerton, near Salisbury, where he spent the rest of his short life. He wrote prolifically, his hymns still being popular throughout the English-speaking world. His treatise, 'The Country Parson,' on the priestly life and his poetry, especially 'The Temple,' earned Herbert a leading place in English literature. He died in 1633.

Reflection

One of my regrets is not having given more time to the reading of poetry. Perhaps because at school we had to learn great chunks of it without either exploring its meaning or beauty, I gave it a miss in any real sense until quite recently when through a compilation of poems produced for Lent, Passiontide and Easter I began to find my way back to it and George Herbert (and to a lesser extent John Donne) provided the door. Much of what I read I still don't understand and the ideas and concepts often prove beyond me but from time to time a phrase or even a word stands out and I am stirred by its beauty or depth of meaning. George Herbert does this more than most and I am so glad that a number of his poems are now used as hymns for contemplation and worship. Like many poets of faith he looks for God in "every corner," "espying the heavens through glass," "sweeping a room," "seven whole days not one in seven". Thus he both lifts us above the mundane to the sublime and brings the sublime to the mundane. I suspect I will never be a poet and may only scratch the surface of great poetry but for that which has brought me to a deeper awareness of God and a deeper wonder of all that He has made I am grateful.

So:

How has poetry spoken to you?

Do you ever read hymns rather than sing them?

Prayer

> Come, my Way, my Truth, my Life:
> Such a way as gives us breath;
> Such a truth as ends all strife,
> Such a life as killeth death.
>
> Come, my Light, my Feast, my Strength:
> Such a light as shows a feast,
> Such a feast as mends in length,
> Such a strength as makes his guest.
>
> Come, my Joy, my Love, my Heart:
> Such a joy as none can move,
> Such a love as none can part,
> Such a heart as joys in love.

George Herbert

January 28th ~ Thomas Aquinas

Thomas Aquinas has been described as the greatest thinker and teacher of the medieval church. Born at Rocca Secca, near Aquino in Italy, Thomas was educated first by the Benedictines at Monte Cassino and then at the University of Naples. Against his family's wishes he joined the mendicant Dominican Order of Preachers. His profound theological wisdom and capacity to impart this, as well in homilies as in hymns, along with his gentleness of spirit in dealing with all, earned him the title "the angelic doctor". He died en route to the Council of Lyons, and his feast has been celebrated on this day since 1970.

Reflection

It is sometimes said that theologians are simply dry, ivory-towered academics trying to answer the questions that no-one else is asking. Well that may be true of some but it certainly wasn't true of Thomas Aquinas nor of most theologians I have met. Rather through their thought out apologia for the Christian faith they enable Christians to have confidence in The Gospel themselves and in sharing it with others. They remind us too that whilst Christianity may be beyond reason it is not unreasonable, that truth matters and that believing is a matter of the mind as well as the heart or the feelings. In these days when it appears to some that in this country at least the Christian faith is under attack as never before the thought out arguments that people like Thomas Aquinas in his generation and C.S. Lewis in ours provide are powerful weapons with which to fight in humility and love and for which we should be grateful.

So:

How reasonable is your faith?

What arguments would you offer for the truth and truths of Christianity?

Prayer

Give me O Lord, a steadfast heart
which no unworthy affection may drag downwards.
Give me an unconquered heart
which no tribulation can wear out.
Give me an upright heart
which no unworthy purpose may tempt aside.
Bestow upon me also, O Lord my God,
understanding to know Thee,
diligence to seek Thee,
wisdom to find Thee,
and a faithfulness that may finally embrace Thee;
through Jesus Christ our Lord.
Amen

Thomas Aquinas

January 29th ~ George Barnes

George Barnes was born in West Bromwich in 1915 and died in Stourbridge in 2002. His career was spent in teaching history and for 63 years he was a Methodist Local Preacher.

Reflection

Having wanted to be a minister since the age of 4 I was glad to be taking part in services from an early age! When I was 13 I joined the Circuit Youth Team who led worship under the watchful eye of George Barnes and when I was placed On Note aged 16 I was delighted that George was appointed as my mentor - even though at our first service together I was nearly killed when someone threw a brick through the window behind the pulpit! I owe so much to George. He taught me how to construct orders of service that "flowed" and sermons that had a pattern to them. He gave me my head to try different things, his only concern being that it should be the best I could offer and thus enable others to offer their best to the glory of God. He introduced me to a theology that was not my own but did it with care and understanding so that I was able to explore rather than feel threatened and he modelled for me the immense privilege of being a preacher of The Gospel. He also gave me a deep love for history, but that's another story! To conduct his funeral service was an enormous privilege but in more ways than one I couldn't have done it without him! How much the church owes to the many "George Barnes" of this world.

So:

When did you last thank a Local Preacher for their ministry in person or with a card, phone call or email?

In what sense is God calling you to preach?

Prayer

> *Grant to us, O Lord, ears to hear your voice,*
> *eyes to see your beauty*
> *and hearts to love your name,*
> *so that hearing, seeing and loving*
> *we may come at last to the joys of your kingdom:*
> *through Christ our Lord.*
> *Amen*
>
> *Christina Rossetti*

January 30ᵗʰ ~ John Bunyan and Terry Waite

Born at Elstow in Bedfordshire in 1628, John Bunyan was largely self-educated and used the Bible as his grammar. He read very few other books, yet he produced Pilgrim's Progress, probably the most original text of spiritual genius that century, telling the story of a Christian on his journey through life to God. It was not written while he was a prisoner in Bedford gaol, as often stated, but during a confinement some years later. He died in 1688.

Terry Waite was born in 1939 in Bollington, Cheshire. He was an Assistant and Envoy for the then Archbishop of Canterbury, Robert Runcie and in the 1980s travelled to Lebanon to try to secure the release of four hostages, including the journalist John McCarthy. He was himself kidnapped and held captive from 1987 to 1991.

He is president of the charity Y Care International (the YMCA's international development and relief agency) and patron of Hostage UK and The Butler Trust. He is also president of Emmaus UK, a charity for homeless people.

Reflection

Pilgrim's Progress was one of the first books I remember reading. Even in the children's edition it's a pretty scary story with its description of the City of Destruction, The Slough of Despair, Vanity Fair, Doubting Castle and the like, as well as characters such as Wordly Wiseman, Apollyon, Lord Hategood and Flatterer who seem determined to divert, deceive and deride Christian on his journey towards the Celestial City. Yet with the help of Evangelist and other faithful companions along the way he eventually arrives "and great was the rejoicing on the other side". Yet for Bunyan these places and people were not simply names in a book but were rooted in his own experience. Terry Waite in our own day might not have used the language of "hobgoblins or foul fiends" as Bunyan did in his famous hymn but he also knew the privations of imprisonment and the testing of his faith as he so vividly illustrated when I met him in London and again in Newcastle a few years ago. Yet both of them had an "evangelist". For John Bunyan it was The Bible, for Terry Waite The Book of Common Prayer, and both had faithful companions who prayed for them and accompanied them in spirit if not in body. Like Christian before them they too eventually came to their "promised land" and through their difficult and dangerous journey have inspired so many on theirs.

So:

How easy or difficult do you find it to be a Christian?

Who has inspired you to keep going?

Prayer

Who would true valour see,
let him come hither;
one here will constant be,
come wind, come weather;
there's no discouragement
shall make him once relent
his first avowed intent
to be a pilgrim.

Since Lord thou dost defend
us with thy spirit,
we know we at the end
shall life inherit.
Then fancies fly away,
we'll fear not what men say;
we'll labour night and day
to be a pilgrim.

John Bunyan

One of St Columba's monks from the monastery of Iona, Aidan was sent as a missionary to Northumbria at the request of King Oswald. Consecrated Bishop of Lindisfarne in 635, Aidan worked closely with Oswald and became involved with the training of priests. From the island of Lindisfarne he was able to combine a monastic lifestyle with missionary journeys to the mainland where, through his concern for the poor and enthusiasm for preaching, he won popular support. This enabled him to strengthen the Church beyond the boundaries of Northumbria. He died in the year 651.

Cuthbert was probably born in the Scottish lowlands around the year 640. One night he saw in the sky a dazzling light and angels carrying a soul up to heaven and resolved to dedicate his life to God. Later he became aware that on that same night Aidan his predecessor had died. Some years later Cuthbert came to Melrose Abbey asking to be admitted as a monk. It was from here that he began his missionary work, which he continued from Lindisfarne when he became Abbot there. Consecrated bishop in 685 he remained an indefatigable traveller and preacher, walking all over his diocese, and spending time as a hermit on The Farne Islands in between. After only a year however he was taken ill and died on Farne in the company of a few of his monks. His tomb is in the feretory in Durham Cathedral.

Reflection

As I prepare to return to the north-east at the end of my Sabbatical it would be inconceivable if I didn't include Aidan and Cuthbert among "my" saints. When I first moved to the north-east 18 years ago it didn't take me long to realise that unless I understood the huge impact that Aidan and Cuthbert had had on the area and upon the development of Christianity, it would be difficult to minister effectively. So many churches named after them, the special place that Holy Island and The Lindisfarne Gospels have, the characteristic use of silence in prayers and the love of hymns from the Celtic tradition all point to something that has sunk deep into the consciousness of the region. But of all the numerous stories told about Aidan and Cuthbert I remember particularly today the way they also went back - Aidan to establish the Christian faith in Northumbria even though all previous initiatives had failed and Cuthbert who returned from his solitary life on The Farne Islands to become Bishop of Lindisfarne. It couldn't have been easy, but then going back rarely is whether to work, to apologise, to learn from past mistakes or to keep returning to tough places and situations out of love for God and others. But pilgrimage requires it of us so that we may better go forward on the journey of faith. Aidan and Cuthbert inspire me to do that today in confidence and hope.

So:

Who or what have you "gone back" for?

What influence does a local saint have on your community or your faith?

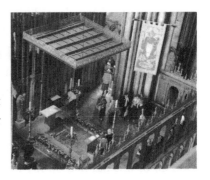

Prayer

Everlasting God, you sent Aidan to proclaim the gospel in this land: and called your servant Cuthbert from following the flock to follow your Son and to be a shepherd of your people: in your mercy, grant that we, following their examples, may bring those who are lost home to your fold, through Christ our Lord.
Amen

February 1st ~ and many others

"There isn't enough time for me to speak of ...." (Hebrews 11 v32)

Reflection

I have been enriched by my reflections on Saints Along The Way during the past two months. Some saints of course were very familiar to me and I have been grateful to recall their memory and to honour their witness and its impact upon me. Of others I knew a little but have been inspired as I have learnt more. But of a number I was quite unaware. Yet as I have reflected on each of their lives I have been conscious again of the different ways in which God uses men and women, of the rich heritage of which I am a part and that with all God's people I am also called a saint and called to live like one.

Yet I have also become aware of the many others I could have included in this book if time and space had permitted and have sometimes had to make difficult decisions as to who to put in and who to leave out. But I am deeply thankful for them all. And there are others who have slipped my memory but who may come back into my mind as days pass and I will value them afresh. But then there are those who I have never known or heard of. Some have been praying for me personally or because of my role or because prayer for all God's people is their special ministry. I am still ambivalent about praying to the saints but have become more and more sure that the saints on earth and in heaven are praying for me and have felt embraced and valued by them all. What influence for good or for God all of this has had on my life and ministry only eternity will tell but in this place and at this time I stand humbled, thankful and richly blessed.

So:

Of all the saints we have reflected on during these past days which one stands out for you? Why?

Have your reflections on the saints enabled you to live like one?

Prayer

For all the saints who from their labours rest,
who Thee by faith before the world confessed,
Thy name, O Jesus, be for ever blest:
Alleluia, alleluia

Thou wast their rock, their fortress and their might;
Thou, Lord, their captain in the well-fought fight;
Thou in the darkness still their one true light:
Alleluia, alleluia!

O blest communion, fellowship divine!
We feebly struggle, they in glory shine;
yet all are one in Thee, for all are Thine:
Alleluia, alleluia!

And when the strife is fierce, the warfare long,
steals on the ear the distant triumph song,
and hearts are brave again, and arms are strong:
Alleluia, alleluia!

From earth's wide bounds, from ocean's farthest coast,
through gates of pearl streams in the countless host,
singing to Father, Son, and Holy Ghost:
Alleluia, alleluia!

William Walsham How

February 2nd ~ Candlemas

This day marks the completion of forty days since the birth of Jesus, when Mary and Joseph took the child to the Temple in Jerusalem. The requirement in Levitical law was for Mary to be 'cleansed', the completion of her purification following the birth of a male child. Until that day she could touch no holy thing nor enter the sanctuary. Yet on seeing the holy family, Simeon praised God and acclaimed the infant as 'the light to enlighten the nations' and the prophet Anna gave thanks and proclaimed him her Redeemer. The image of Christ as the Light has led to the celebration of light overcoming darkness, with candles often taking a central place in the worship of this day.

Reflection

My reflections on Saints Along the Way began surrounded by Candles in Norwich Cathedral on Advent Sunday and they end surrounded by more candles in Durham Cathedral at Candlemas - truly a journey of light from light!

Now the candles that have been burning brightly these past two months are extinguished. They were lit as the days were growing shorter and darker, they are extinguished as the days are growing longer and brighter yet in every changing season and in every changing scene of life the true light remains. He shines out through saints like Simeon and Anna who watched and waited faithfully until they saw God's promises fulfilled. He shines out whenever love conquers hate, hope overcomes despair and life defeats death. He shines out in all who walk in the light as they follow Jesus their crucified and risen Lord. As the journey continues may all whom the Spirit lights give light to the world so that we and all God's children shall be free and the whole earth live to praise His name.

So:

What does it mean for you to give light to the world?

What is ending and beginning for you today? Offer it to God.

Prayer

Lord, you fulfilled the hope of Simeon and Anna,
who lived to welcome the Messiah:
may we, who have received your gift beyond words,
prepare to meet Christ Jesus when He comes
to bring us to eternal life:
for He is alive and reigns, now and for ever.
Amen

Acknowledgements

I am most grateful to The Society of Saint Francis for permission to use the paragraphs with which many of the entries begin. Where I am aware copyright exists the details are as follows:-

Wild Goose Resources Group, Iona Community Reproduced with Permission * Introduction
Central Board of Finance of The Church of England Permission sought * December 1st, 4th, 7th, 23rd, 24th, 25th, 28th, 29th * January 1st, 2nd, 19th, 21st, 26th, 31st * February 2nd
The Book of a Thousand Prayers 1996 Compiled by Angela Ashwin Reproduced with permission * December 2nd, 6th, 16th, 21st, 22nd, 26th, 27th * January 3rd, 4th, 6th, 10th, 11th, 13th, 22nd, 28th
The SPCK Book of Christian Prayer 1995 Reproduced with Permission * December 8th, 9th, 10th, 13th, 15th * Jaunary 12th, 14th, 16th, 24th
Make Way Music Reproduced with permission * Jan 20th

Image Permissions

Unless specified below, all images used are in the public domain or have been used with permission where no attribution is needed.

Cover	Copyright © widehdwalls.com. Used with permission.
p 4	Copyright © Ian Capper via geograph.org.uk (cc) BY-SA 2.0
p 7	Copyright © rgbstock.com. Used with permission.
p 8	18th century icon. Public domain. Current location: Iconostasis of Transfiguration Church, Kizhi Monastery, Karelia, Russia.
p 10	(i) 17th century painting. Public domain. Current location: Kobe City Museum
p 11	(ii) Copyright © freeworldmaps.net. Used with permission.
p 12	Copyright © Aidan Hart. Used with permission.
p 14	Copyright © Leo Osborn. Used with permission.
p 16	From the Public Papers of the Presidents of the United States. Public domain.
p 18	Copyright © Bjoertvedt (cc) BY-SA 3.0
p 20	Copyright © Fr. Andrew Phillips/Orthodox England. Used with permission.
p 22	Copyright © vegansoldier (cc) BY-SA 2.0
p 24	Copyright © Photograph of Thomas Merton by John Howard Griffin. Used with permission of the Merton Legacy Trust and the Thomas Merton Center at Bellarmine University.
p 26	Copyright © Leo Osborn. Used with permission.
p 28	Public Domain
p 30	1772 Painting by Joshua Reynolds. Public domain.
p 32	(i) 1656 Painting by Francisco de Zurbarán. Public domain. Current location: Archdiocesan Museum in Katowice
p 32	(ii) 1615 Painting by Peter Paul Rubens. Public domain. Current location: Kunsthistorisches Museum
p 34	Public domain.
p 35	Copyright © National Library of Scotland (cc) BY-NC-SA 2.5 UK: Scotland
p 36	Copyright © Leo Osborn. Used with permission.

p 74	14th/15th Century Icon. Public Domain.
p 76	Copyright © Maria Gkinala. Used with permission.
p 79	Copyright © Raimond Spekking (cc) BY-SA 3.0
p 80	c. 1560 Painting by Juan de Juanes. Public Domain. Current Location: Museum of Santiago de Compostela
p 81	Copyright © Vasco Roxo (cc) BY-SA 2.0
p 82	Public Domain
p 84	(i) Copyright © The Christian Hall of Fame, Canton Baptist Temple, Canton, Ohio. Used with permission.
p 84	(ii) Copyright © Jenny Sinclair. Used with permission.
p 86	c. 1636 painting by Sir Anthony Van Dyck. Public domain. Current Location: National Portrait Gallery
p 88	Copyright © Debbie Talbert. Used with permission.
p 90	(i) c. 1140 manuscript possibly written by Aelred. Public domain.
p 90	(ii) Copyright © David Nashford. Used with permission.
p 92	Public Domain
p 94	Copyright © Wolfgang Richter. Used with permission.
p 96	Copyright © Richard English. Used with permission.
p 98	(i) Copyright © Mike Dixon. Used with permission.
p 98	(ii) Portrait by Raymond Lynde. Copyright © Royal Norfolk Regimental Museum. Used with permission.
p 98	(iii) Copyright © National Portrait Gallery (cc) BY-NC-ND 3.0
p 98	(iv) Illumination in Margery Kempe's manuscripts. Public Domain.
p 100	Copyright © Rept0n1x (cc) BY-SA 3.0
p 102	Copyright © freeimages.com. Used with permission.
p 103	Copyright © WCC. Used with permission.
p 104	Copyright © Mr. Christopher Guy, Worcester Cathedral Archaeologist. Reproduced by permission of the Chapter of Worcester Cathedral (U.K.)
p 106	Copyright © Bobbie Hanvey (cc) BY 3.0
p 108	Copyright © Fratelli Bonella. Used with permission.
p 110	Stained glass window in the Franciscan church in Szombathely, Hungary. Public domain.

Lightning Source UK Ltd.
Milton Keynes UK
UKOW06f0826161015

260669UK00009B/29/P